Edward Schillebeeckx and Interreligious Dialogue

Edward Schillebeeckx
and Interreligious Dialogue
Perspectives from Asian Theology

EDMUND KEE-FOOK CHIA

☙PICKWICK *Publications* · Eugene, Oregon

EDWARD SCHILLEBEECKX AND INTERRELIGIOUS DIALOGUE
Perspectives from Asian Theology

Copyright © 2012 Edmund Kee-Fook Chia. All rights reserved. Except for brief quotations in critical publications or reviews, no part of this book may be reproduced in any manner without prior written permission from the publisher. Write: Permissions, Wipf and Stock Publishers, 199 W. 8th Ave., Suite 3, Eugene, OR 97401.

Pickwick Publications
An Imprint of Wipf and Stock Publishers
199 W. 8th Ave., Suite 3
Eugene, OR 97401

www.wipfandstock.com

ISBN 13: 978-1-61097-115-7

Cataloguing-in-Publication data:

Chia, Edmund Kee-Fook.

Edward Schillebeeckx and interreligious dialogue : perspectives from Asian theology / Edmund Kee-Fook Chia.

xii + 166 p. ; 23 cm. Includes bibliographical references.

ISBN 13: 978-1-61097-115-7

1. Schillebeeckx, Edward, 1914–2009. 2. Dialogue—Religious aspects. 3. Christianity—Asia. I. Title.

BX4705 S51314 C35 2012

Manufactured in the U.S.A.

*For all the wonderful people at
Catholic Theological Union
(students, staff, and faculty)*

Contents

Foreword by Robert J. Schreiter, CPPS / *ix*

Introduction / 1

1 Interreligious Dialogue and the Church's Teachings / 9

2 Religious Pluralism and Asian Theology / 27

3 Schillebeeckx's Theology: Context and Influence / 46

4 Schillebeeckx's Theology: Approach and Method / 64

5 Schillebeeckx's Trilogy: Theology of *Dominus Iesus* / 83

6 Towards Schillebeeckx's Theology of Dialogue / 110

7 Toward an Asian Theology of Dialogue / 127

Conclusion / 151

Bibliography / 159

Foreword

ROBERT J. SCHREITER, CPPS[1]

ONE ISSUE MORE THAN any other stands at the center of theological agenda today: what do the Christian claims about what God has done for the world in Jesus Christ mean vis-à-vis the other great religious traditions present in the world today? Many of these traditions—Hinduism, Buddhism, and some of the other religions of India—predate Christianity. Another, Islam, now constitutes the largest religious body in the world after Christianity itself. The presence and the persistence of these traditions raise a question that goes beyond the claims made by Christians about salvation in Jesus Christ. These other great religious traditions hold before us what is now called a theology of religious pluralism. They cause Christians to ask: what role do all these religious traditions play in God's larger plan for the world? Christianity grew by leaps and bounds in numbers during the twentieth century. But at that century's end, Christians constituted still the same percentage of the world's population (about 34 percent) they did before the missionary endeavors since 1900. Christians have worked very hard, simply to maintain its place. On this basis it seems foolish for Christians to think that these other traditions are now going to fade away. One of them—Islam—is today growing faster than Christianity. So how do we give a theological account for what we see happening around us?

---

1. A student of Edward Schillebeeckx in the 1970s, Schreiter is one of the foremost scholars of Schillebeeckx's theology. He was the first to hold the University of Nijmegen's Chair for Theology and Culture, sponsored by the Schillebeeckx Foundation. He serves as Vatican II Professor of Theology at Catholic Theological Union in Chicago.

It is becoming increasingly clear that responding to the question of religious pluralism—God's plan for the world in the light of Christianity among the other great religious traditions of the world—could well have consequences as dramatic for the Christian faith as did those of the great christological controversies of the fourth and fifth centuries. At that time, the question was the nature of Jesus Christ's own person as related to God in his divinity and to us in his humanity. Existing philosophical categories were not capable of articulating biblical faith. And so those categories, taken from the Hellenistic world, had to be redefined to carry the biblical meanings that the Church needed to maintain its faith. Even then, those redefined categories—such as being (*ousia*), nature (*physis*), and person (*hypostasis*)—caused confusion when they were taken outside the language and culture of Hellenism into the Syriac and Coptic worlds. Despite the best intentions, they led to breakdowns in communication and divisions among the churches that were not entirely acknowledged until fifteen hundred years later.

Today, it is the *work* of Christ (rather than his person) that has become the prime theological challenge. How do we witness faithfully to and communicate Christian faith in Christ and what God has done in Christ for the world, amid the continuing presence of other ways of relating to the Transcendent? The challenge reaches this time beyond the territories surrounding the Mediterranean—they extend to the entire world, and especially to Asia. One thing that is becoming increasingly clear is that the categories that have shaped Western Christianity are, by themselves, not likely to be completely adequate to carry and articulate Christian faith in a religiously plural world. This has been the message coming out of Asia now for nearly half a century, where Christianity, as a minority faith, needs to be presented in ways that are at once true to its heritage and commitments yet are also able to speak in ways that are intelligible and credible to other great faith traditions.

Few theologians today are more acutely aware of this than Edmund Chia, the author of the book before you. Himself Malaysian and Catholic Christian, he served for eight years as the Executive Secretary of Ecumenical and Interfaith Relations for the Federation of Asian Bishops' Conferences. There he had daily experience of the challenge of presenting Christian faith in a religiously plural world. As such, he speaks as a credible witness both to the effort in Asia to give an account of Christianity and to respectfully and authentically engage members of other religious traditions in Asia.

His point of departure in this study is the Vatican declaration *Dominus Iesus*, a collection of extracts from authentic teaching on the salvific meaning of Christ and the place of the Church, issued by the Congregation for the Doctrine of the Faith in 2000. The reactions that met this document—both within and outside the Catholic Church—indicated how neuralgic these issues had become. The reaction from Asia, which Chia documents here, may affirm the good intentions behind the document but nevertheless point to its inadequacy, both in its composition and its presentation. If nothing else, *Dominus Iesus* pointed to the huge challenge that the Catholic Church—and indeed, all of Christianity—faces in coming to terms with this great theological conundrum.

Chia is too perceptive and knowledgeable a theologian to presume to be able to fully outline (let alone settle) the issues involved. Rather, what he does in this helpful study is to examine the potential contribution of one Western theologian, Edward Schillebeeckx, to addressing these challenges from the point of view of Western Christianity. Schillebeeckx himself never visited Asia, but a number of younger scholars from Asia have shown him to have been uniquely sensitive to emerging issues in the world church. His experience as an informal advisor to many bishops at the Second Vatican Council, and his engagement with theologians from around the world through his leadership in the international theological journal *Concilium*, made him as sensitive to the theological issues of the world church as any European theologian of his generation. Consequently, his work has been called upon by the emerging generation of theologians to address issues arising in the Church around the world.

What Chia offers us here is an unfolding of Schillebeeckx's methods and perspectives as they are brought to bear on the theology of religious pluralism today. Schillebeeckx's contribution is by no means the definitive one. But he does represent an important bridge between Western and Asian theologies; one that is expressed in categories Western theologians can understand, but also one that allows Asian theologians such as Chia to begin to present new ways to mediate Asian Christian experience on the question of religious pluralism to the wider world church. In so doing, this book provides an important step that can bring Western and Asian thinking about this crucial question into closer communication. We all owe a debt of gratitude to Edmund Chia for taking this step. There are few people better situated to do this than he. It is the kind of work we all need if we are to come to terms with what is shaping up to be the single greatest theological challenge to Christianity in the twenty-first century.

Robert Schreiter, CPPS
Catholic Theological Union, Chicago, USA

Introduction

> In those final days, he made the remark that, for him, the best image of God that human beings could muster was God as light. In the late morning on December 23, 2009, he said, "I see so much light!" Around two in the afternoon, Edward said: "God is calling me!" These were his last words. Around 5:15, he uttered a gentle sigh, and he was gone. He died a grace-filled death, after a life of proclaiming a God who is so near to us.[1]

THAT DECEMBER 23 WAS just a day or two after the winter solstice, which marks the beginning of longer daylight in the Northern hemisphere, is significant in the obituary above. Edward Schillebeeckx, who lived all his life in Europe, specifically in the Low Countries, was certainly seeing that extra light of the late morning sun with the eyes of flesh. With the eyes of mind, however, he saw the light as not only representing the reversal of seasons but also God as light. This, to be sure, is the same God whom he had been preaching and proclaiming as light of the world throughout his entire life and whom he saw in his prayer and meditation through the eyes of spirit.

SCHILLEBEECKX'S LIFE AND CONTRIBUTION

Ranked amongst the theological giants of the twentieth century, Edward Cornelius Florentius Schillebeeckx may have left us at the age of ninety-five, but his relevance and significance remain. Immediate testimony to this is that, following his death, obituaries appeared in numerous newspapers around the world, from the *Daily Telegraph* to the *New York Times* to the *Guardian Weekly* to the *National Catholic Reporter* and the *Union of Catholic Asian News*. Further evidence is that dozens of books have been published about the man and his thoughts and more than seventy-five dissertations written on his theology. Moreover, these books have found

---

1. Schreiter, "In Memoriam," lines 155–65.

their way to more than fifteen hundred libraries throughout the world and some have seen more than a dozen editions and been translated into several languages.

Like his name, which is long and difficult to pronounce, his books are also not easy to read or understand. Not only because of their length (a book he published in 1977 numbered 925 pages!) but also because they are frequently laced with profound scientific, philosophical, and theological vocabulary and ideas. We might note here that the Edward Schillebeeckx Foundation (established in his honor by the Dutch community and the Dominican Order to which he belonged) is already at work in producing a massive eleven-volume English translation of his theological writings, including the hundreds of sermons he preached over the half century he was in active ministry.

Born in Belgium at the beginning of the First World War and encountering the disjunction of the Second World War just as he was entering into the world of theology, it comes as no surprise that Schillebeeckx's theology reveals a sense of tentativeness and at times even a sense of vulnerability. He would later assert that there is no such thing as absoluteness in life, including in religion or theology. His focus, therefore, has always been on the pastoral and personal nature of theology and that they should relate to and affect life and not deal so much with abstract metaphysical concepts and dogmas, many of which are expressed in absolutist terms. Theology, he insists, has to be life changing and, for that to happen, must lead to action. Such a theology begins with the concrete experiences of people on the ground and is engaged in with the hope that the praxis engendered helps to usher in the coming reign of God.

Coming to prominence in the period surrounding the Second Vatican Council and like *Gaudium et Spes*, which opened the Church to the wider world community, Schillebeeckx saw himself propelled into the international arena as a theologian of not only the Catholic or European communities but that of the whole world as well. By the mid-1960s the name Schillebeeckx was almost synonymous with the progress and transformation set into motion by Vatican II. Indeed, at the heights of his career he was receiving invitations for lecture tours across Europe and North America. Upon reaching the end of his teaching career at the University of Nijmegen in the Netherlands, he was awarded the prestigious Erasmus Prize in 1982 for his contribution towards European culture in general, the first and only theologian to have been so honored. He continued to be active in research, writing, and ministry after that, and by the end of his life had several dozen books and more than four hundred essays to his name.

As the first Roman Catholic theologian to engage in biblical exegesis and the historical-critical method, Schillebeeckx played a key role in helping bridge the traditional and older Neo-Scholastic method of doing theology of the nineteenth century to the hermeneutical and phenomenological approaches of the twentieth century. His critical scholarship was applied not only to Scripture but to exploring the development of the Church and its doctrines as well. This pioneering move was to become a significant influence to Catholic theologians all over and especially those theologizing in the developing world. With the endorsement of Vatican II, Third World theologians then embarked on a journey of no return, employing the hermeneutical-critical method that Schillebeeckx promoted as a primary approach and method for *doing* theology. This method insists that theology does not remain merely a repetition of or a tweaking of traditional theological formulae. Instead, it insists that theology is a serious discipline of contemplative discernment through a mutually critical correlation and even confrontation between Scripture and tradition, on the one hand, and contemporary experience and the social and cultural realities, on the other.

Considering experience as starting point for theological reflection was a novelty amongst Catholic theologians in the 1950s and 1960s. But because Schillebeeckx believed that the Word of God is a living Word and that God is new every moment, he insisted that the people's and communities' experience should constitute a primary resource for all theologizing. He even went so far as to say that theology is but an interpretation of God's Word, including the theology of Nicaea and Chalcedon or that of the New Testament. His method, therefore, advances the need for a reflection on not only contemporary experience but the experience of the Christian communities of the fourth and fifth centuries—from which the christological doctrines evolved—as well as the experience of the early Christians—from which the gospels and New Testament epistles issued forth. This, Schillebeeckx posits, is the hermeneutical situation, and every theologian has to be cognizant of it.

GENESIS AND THRUST OF THE BOOK

My own association with Schillebeeckx began when I went to Nijmegen to pursue doctoral studies in intercultural theology. While privileged to have my heart personally seized by the gentle warmth and unassuming nature of this theological giant, it was his views and ideas that captured my mind and intellect. Taking his advice that the starting point of theology is our own experience, I began to reflect on my own upbringing of having grown up as a Christian living in multireligious Malaysia. I decided, therefore, that the focus of my research would be the phenomenon of religious pluralism. The decision was not difficult, as I had for a number of years been actively involved in the ministry of interreligious dialogue for the Church in Asia, having served as Executive Secretary of Interreligious Dialogue for the Federation of Asian Bishops' Conferences.

But the most immediate and precipitating reason for my choosing the topic was the release of the Vatican Declaration *Dominus Iesus* in the year 2000, just as I was beginning my studies. Reviews and commentaries indicate that the declaration was targeted at Asian theologians, in particular those promoting a theology of religious pluralism. The declaration was further viewed as part of a larger and ongoing conversation between officials in Rome and theologians in Asia, in what has come to be known as a creative tension between the "center" and the "periphery." This tension is viewed as the inevitable dialectic resulting from the renewal of the Second Vatican Council. My task therefore was to reflect on the dynamics behind this creative tension to discern how we can better appreciate the different approaches of theology taken by those in Rome and those in Asia. To that end I turned to Schillebeeckx.

In particular it was Schillebeeckx's theological methodologies that I found myself exploring. But before doing so it was important to begin by visiting his contextual, philosophical, and theological influences. That he himself underwent a transformation from the neo-scholastic method to the hermeneutical-critical method upon encountering the postmodern and post-religious Europe in the 1960s, and that he himself, along with the Dutch Church, was embroiled in the center-periphery tension as a result of this transformation, served as heuristic for appreciating the dynamics taking place between Rome and Asia.

It is interesting to note that the experience of Schillebeeckx and of the Dutch Church has parallels to the experience of the Asian Church and its theologians of today. The significant difference is that the former took place soon after the closing session of Vatican II and involved people living much closer to Rome, the center of Roman Catholicism, while the latter began about twenty or thirty years later and continues to be played out today in a continent far away from the center. It is also interesting to note that both the Dutch episcopate and the Asian bishops stood firmly behind their theologians in responding to the inquiries of the Vatican's Congregation for the Doctrine of the Faith. As with Schillebeeckx, the Asian theologians who came under investigation served as regular consultants of the Asian bishops.

A more important point of interest is that the issues raised by the Vatican declaration *Dominus Iesus*, which are central to the center-periphery dynamics involving the Church in Asia today, have actually been addressed by Schillebeeckx one way or another. Issues pertaining to the uniqueness and universality of Jesus Christ were explored by Schillebeeckx in his first book, *Jesus*. The meanings and understandings of salvation in relation to Christ's uniqueness and universality were central to Schillebeeckx's second volume of the trilogy, *Christ*. The mission of the Church and its relation with the world and with other religions were the topics of investigation in Schillebeeckx's ecclesiological volume, *Church*. In other words, the central concerns of *Dominus Iesus*, especially those that arose in light of the phenomenon of religious pluralism (for example, the threat of relativism), have all been addressed by Schillebeeckx in his various works.

Hence, the thrust of this book is Schillebeeckx's theology, especially how he reflects on the Church's role in light of religious pluralism. Specifically, his theology, distilled from his christological trilogy—*Jesus: An Experiment in Christology*; *Christ: The Christian Experience in the Modern World*; and *Church: The Human Story of God*—is juxtaposed against the Vatican declaration *Dominus Iesus*. The focus will be on how he—and *Dominus Iesus*—responds to the *christological* question of "Who do you say that I am?" (the *Jesus* book), the *soteriological* question of "What does salvation from God in Jesus mean to us?" (the *Christ* book), and the *ecclesiological* question of "What is the Church's response to this offer of salvation?" (the *Church* book). It is in this sense that the trilogy can also be seen as Schillebeeckx's own proclamation of the Lord Jesus, or his very own *Dominus Iesus*.

ORGANIZATION AND STRUCTURE OF THE BOOK

We begin this book by exploring the critical urgency of interreligious dialogue in contemporary society. Chapter 1 looks at this against the backdrop of conflicts and divisions perpetuated in the name of religion. In this regard, even as the Church has advanced in its attitude towards other religions certain teachings remain ambiguous at best. In particular, the Vatican declaration *Dominus Iesus* will be examined and the reactions and responses to it sketched out. These will then be discussed in the context of the renewal and irruptions set into motion by the Second Vatican Council.

The second chapter discusses the second of such major irruptions, viz., theologies that attend to the phenomenon of religious pluralism. It explores how and why *Dominus Iesus* is seen as a document promulgated in the wake of the advent of Asian theologies of religious pluralism. Three case studies are presented as antecedents to the Vatican declaration and illustrating the center-periphery dynamics going on between the Church in Rome and the Church in Asia. The chapter concludes by advocating an inculturated theology for Asian Christians that is at once faithful to the Christian tradition as well as sensitive to the Asian cultural context.

Before venturing into this Asian theology an appropriate theological methodology has to be discerned to assist in the task of inculturation. For this purpose Schillebeeckx's method is adopted, for its freshness and relevance to contemporary visions of theology. In keeping with his own thesis that contextual realities are significant sources of theology, chapter 3 looks at Schillebeeckx's own philosophical and theological formation, especially in light of the experiences surrounding the Dutch Church and amidst the renewal of the Second Vatican Council.

Chapter 4 focuses specifically on issues of theological methodology. First, it looks at the development of the scholastic and then the neo-scholastic influence on theology and especially the latter's impact on Schillebeeckx. Next, it discusses the period that led to Schillebeeckx's momentous turn around, resulting in his adoption of the principles of hermeneutics. These principles are explored and then extended to include elements of critical theory, with its emphasis on an option for the marginalized and a mandate for orthopraxis.

The fifth chapter turns its focus on the essential elements of Schillebeeckx's theology. It outlines his christological trilogy and shows how his aim of proclaiming Jesus as Lord is accomplished in the three volumes. The significance of this is that he manages to do this by being respectful of and sensitive to modern culture and especially religions other than Christianity. It is here we note that in his "Jesus books" he addresses most of the critical christological and ecclesiological issues raised by the Vatican declaration *Dominus Iesus*.

Chapter 6 begins with a quick comparison between the Vatican's *Dominus Iesus* and Schillebeeckx's theology to look at their tone and thrust. It then examines in greater detail the essential characteristics of the latter, or what Schillebeeckx himself calls the "conjunctural" elements of his theology. This sets the stage for developing a theology of dialogue, where Schillebeeckx's emphasis on God acting in the world and in history calls for the recognition of the role of other religions in accompanying the Church's mission of ushering in the kingdom of God.

Finally, by the time we get to chapter 7 we are ready to postulate an Asian theology of dialogue as a response to the concerns raised by *Dominus Iesus*, the document that provided the impetus for the present study. With Schillebeeckx's theology and method as the background, we discern how the Asian Church has been addressing the theme of religious pluralism in its theology. This is done by advocating that theology has to be engaged in through the process and spirit of dialogue. An Asian theology of dialogue is a theology that begins with dialogue and ends with the call for more dialogue. As will be seen, a lot of the themes and methods about which Schillebeeckx's theology is emphatic are evident in this Asian theology of dialogue. In a way, this chapter can also be regarded as an "application" of Schillebeeckx's theology.

This Asian theology of dialogue enables the Church to serve, in the words of Schillbeeckx, as a "sacrament of dialogue." It spells out both the opportunity and responsibility for the Church to discover its mission as facilitator of dialogue in today's religiously pluralistic world. Such is the task of not only the Asian Church but the universal Church as well if it wishes to take seriously the challenge of *ecclesia semper purificanda* ("the Church must constantly purify itself"). In playing this role, in the words of Schillebeeckx, "the Church [is] put in its place, as well as given the place which is its due."[2]

---

2. Schillebeeckx, *Church*, xix.

1

Interreligious Dialogue and the Church's Teachings[1]

THE SECOND VATICAN COUNCIL has been regarded as the most significant moment for the Roman Catholic Church since the Protestant Reformation and the Council of Trent. Unlike Trent, which was a reform council, Vatican II was a renewal and updating (*aggiornamento*) council. It was convened by Pope John XXIII for the purpose of encountering the demands of the modern world at a time when the Church was stable and almost at its best. Vatican II was not a doctrinal council to arrest heresies—as was Vatican I (which arrested the threat of modernity) and Trent (which countered the challenges posed by the Protestant Reformation). Instead, it was a renewal council, aimed at bringing about transformation within the Church itself for the sake of self-improvement and to bring it up to speed with the development of the culture that surrounds it.

As a renewal council, Vatican II set the Church on the path to a totally new and fresh outlook, not only in its manifestation but in its thinking and theology as well. The most significant aspect of this is no doubt Catholicism's relations with other religions. It gave rise to what has since been known as "interreligious dialogue." This dialogue ministry takes a variety of forms and engages specific methods. It involves not only the members of the hierarchy but that of the entire community as well. It can also be seen as the Church catching up with the transformations taking place in the modern world and grappling with the fact that the various religions are already encountering one another. This last fact is happening

---

1. A significant portion of this chapter was published as "The Asian Church Dialogues with *Dominus Iesus*" in *SEDOS* 34 (March 2002) 86–94, and also in *Japan Mission Journal* 56 (Spring 2002) 50–63.

not without consequences, some of which are serious while others can even be deadly.

THE URGENT IMPERATIVE OF DIALOGUE

Indeed, interreligious dialogue has become a buzzword in many other facets of life. At this particular moment in history there is no denying its importance and critical necessity, not only for the survival of the religious communities but for the entire world's survival as well. As some has put it, the alternative to dialogue is none other than death. Death, of course, is given expression by the major problem besieging humanity in recent times: conflict and violence, as brought to the fore by the September 11 attack, which was followed soon after by the October 7 attack. September 11 comes to mind for those who regard the "war on America" as the most heinous act committed against humanity. October 7 comes to mind for those who regard the "war on Islam" (beginning with the first DU bombs dropped on Afghanistan in 2001) as abominable and ruthless.

It doesn't help that each side is calling the other "terrorists" and spreading propaganda that incites its population towards hate. The image of the millions of impoverished Muslim farmers, widows, and orphans affected by the bombings as well as the hundreds of thousands who have died on account of the invasion of Afghanistan and Iraq feature most often in the minds of those on one side of the conflict. Likewise, images of violence perpetrated against Western targets, from Bali to Riyadh to Amman to Athens to London, have reached the living rooms of most American and Western homes.

While many will rightly not label this as a war of religions, the numerous cases of backlash against Muslims in America and other Western nations and the violence perpetrated against churches in Muslim nations suggest that there are others who do perceive this, even if wrongly, as the West's war against Islam and vice versa. Unfortunately, the West is also synonymous with Christianity in the minds of some who reside in non-Western nations. Also unfortunate is that the word "Muslim" is very often applied as an adjective whenever the noun "terrorism" is bandied around. The most unfortunate casualty in all this is that the world is being dichotomized, not unlike how Samuel Huntington caricatures the "clash of civilizations," dividing the one sacred world and its people into *us* and *them*, where either word can mean either Muslim or Christian.

This us-versus-them phenomenon does not seem to be abating. If anything, it seems to be on the increase by the day. Conflicts committed in the name of religion have become everyday occurrences in some parts of the world. Enough people have been killed for the sake of religion and enough are also killing in its name. Suffice to say that religious communities have not been appropriately effective in their efforts at containing the fanatical abuse and instrumentalization of religion. This, perhaps, has as much to do with the lack of attention given to promoting positive attitudes towards the beliefs and practices of other religions, as with the lack of opportunities for promoting interactions across the adherents of the different religions. Instead, religious communities are generally parochially minded and wont to keep their followers confined to their own, thus segregating them from believers of other religions. Besides, religious leaders are also wont to proclaiming the superiority of their own religion while at the same time condemning the religions of others, thus reinforcing the us-versus-them mentality.

Aside from these global and macro-level realities, it won't be too far-fetched to suggest that at our base realities, in our local communities and churches, the situation is not significantly better. Even as there may not be interreligious conflicts, one cannot claim that interreligious harmony actually exists. Tolerance and polite coexistence are more likely the prevailing attitudes. In this regard, parishes and religious communities have virtual walls that seem to be keeping their own in and the peoples of other religions out. At times, the parish pastor does not even know the name of the Muslim imam or the Buddhist monk living in the mosque or temple down the road from the church. Thus, not only is the call for the praxis of interreligious dialogue timely and prophetic, it can also help chart out a very different future for the Church. It is hoped that this future would see Christians dismantling the walls of prejudice and segregation in favor of erecting bridges of dialogue, peace, and interreligious camaraderie. Needless to say, a lot of effort needs to be invested if this is to become a reality.

AMBIVALENCE OF THE CHURCH'S TEACHINGS

In addition to the abovementioned global and societal realities urging that interreligious dialogue be enhanced, intraecclesial factors suggesting the same also do abound. In particular, much work still needs to be done by the Church, especially on the official and hierarchical levels, with regard to her attitude towards other religions. Notwithstanding the directions set forth by Vatican II and the many laudable and constructive efforts on the part of Popes Paul VI, John Paul II, and Benedict XVI in reaching out to leaders of other religions, the Church's overall commitment to interreligious dialogue remains ambivalent at best.

Not only have some actions and statements from the Church's hierarchy seemed unsupportive of this mission, they sometimes reveal a Church that is somewhat fearful of it as well, at times even acting in ways that seem to undermine dialogue. The most significant instance in recent times has been the promulgation of the Vatican document entitled *Dominus Iesus*. Released by the Congregation for the Doctrine of the Faith (CDF) on September 5, 2000, *Dominus Iesus* is subtitled "On the Unicity and Salvific Universality of Jesus Christ and the Church." This document actually represents the most recent of the teachings of the Catholic Church specifically on the topic of interreligious dialogue, and for that reason will be employed here as a critical signpost that cannot be ignored. While a lot has and can be written about *Dominus Iesus* (both positive as well as negative), it suffices that we look at some of the key points of antagonism here.

THE VATICAN DECLARATION DOMINUS IESUS

Presented by then-Cardinal Joseph Ratzinger at no less than a press conference, *Dominus Iesus* was said to be drafted in reference to the "contemporary debate on the relationship of Christianity to other religions."[2] Ratzinger immediately points to the crux of the problem, namely, the mistaken notion that "all religions are equally valid ways of salvation for those who follow them." "This is a conviction," Ratzinger regrets, "that is widespread by now not only in theological circles, but also in increasingly broad sectors of public opinion, both Catholic and non-Catholic." Almost in the same breath he unequivocally identifies the source of the problem, namely, "relativism."

"The fundamental consequence of this way of thinking," Ratzinger counsels, is "the substantial rejection of the identification of the individual historical person, Jesus of Nazareth, with the very reality of God, of

---

2. Ratzinger, "Reasons for Claim," line 1. Subsequent quotes in this section are from lines 1–75 of this source.

the living God." Such ideas render dialogue a "radically different meaning from the one intended by Vatican II." Specifically, "dialogue, or better, *the ideology of dialogue*, replaces the *mission* and the *urgency to conversion*: dialogue is no longer the way to discover the truth," claims Ratzinger (emphasis in original text). "Dialogue in the new ideological conceptions," Ratzinger summarizes, "is instead the essence of the relativist 'dogma' and the opposite of both 'conversion' and 'mission.'"

Ratzinger then posits that "such a relativist philosophy is found at the base both of post-metaphysical Western thought and of the negative theology of Asia." "The result," he continues, "is that the figure of Jesus Christ loses his characteristic of unicity and salvific universality." Such relativism can only be "accompanied by a false concept of tolerance," which in turn is "connected with the loss and the renunciation of the issue of truth." "Without a serious claim for truth," Ratzinger advises, "even an appreciation of other religions becomes absurd and contradictory, since one has no criterion to determine what is positive in a religion, distinguishing it from what is negative or the fruit of superstition and deception." While advocating that "everything of beauty and truth that exists in religions must not be lost, but instead must be acknowledged and prized," he cautions, however, that this does not mean we ignore "the errors and deceptions that are nonetheless present in religions."

Ratzinger submits that while religions and cultures have no choice but to meet and so be engaged in dialogue with one another, "this, however, has nothing to do with the abandonment of the claim on the part of the Christian faith to have received as a gift from God in Christ the definitive and complete revelation of the mystery of salvation." More important is that "we must rule out that mentality of indifferentism based on a religious relativism that leads one to think that 'one religion is as good as the other' (*Redemptoris Missio*, 36)." Ratzinger concludes by reiterating that "esteem and respect for the world's religions . . . does not diminish the originality and uniqueness of the revelation of Jesus Christ and does not in any way limit the missionary task of the Church."

Turning to the document *Dominus Iesus* itself, we note a rather ambivalent tone. The document posits its aim is "to recall to Bishops, theologians, and all the Catholic faithful, certain indispensable elements of Christian doctrine" (§3). In this regard it highlights the central concern that the "Church's constant missionary proclamation is endangered today by relativistic theories which seek to justify religious pluralism, not only *de facto* but also *de jure* (or in principle)" (§4). This, of course, appears harmless, since there is certainly nothing wrong with asserting one's own faith identity and warning against plausible pitfalls. But when the document proclaims the "definitive and complete character of the revelation of Jesus Christ" (§5) and then goes on to regard other religions as mere "beliefs," "still in search of the absolute truth and still lacking assent to God" (§7), it probably borders on the boundaries of acceptable interreligious relations. Likewise, it does seem a bit insensitive of *Dominus Iesus* to proclaim that "God has willed that the Church founded by [Jesus Christ] be the instrument for the salvation of all humanity [cf. Acts 17: 30–31]," especially when at the same time it asserts that "though other religions can receive divine grace, it is also certain that objectively speaking they are in a gravely deficient situation" (§22).

Aside from wondering how the document arrived at this "certain" and "objective" truth that other religions are "gravely deficient," one wonders if such a proclamation can objectively reinforce the us-versus-them sentiments and fuel even more interreligious enmity and tension. Indian theologian Michael Amaladoss's advice is appropriate here: "We can be positive in witnessing to our experience of God without presuming to judge the quality of the experience of God of other believers."[3]

THEOLOGICAL ASSERTIONS OF DOMINUS IESUS

The first three chapters of *Dominus Iesus* address the christological issues of the fullness and definitiveness of the revelation of Jesus Christ, his salvific mystery, and the concomitant role of the Holy Spirit. The final three chapters address the ecclesiological issues of the unicity and unity of the Church, its relation to the kingdom of Christ, and its role in the salvation of all, including people of other religions. The latter ecclesiological chapters take the earlier christological chapters as a foundation in a hermeneutics that posits that the unicity and universality of Christ is extended to the unicity and universality of the Church. The parallels or analogies found between the christological and ecclesiological sections lead to the conclusion that since there is only one savior for humankind, viz., Jesus Christ, therefore there is but only one church and this church subsists in the Catholic Church.

---

3. Amaladoss, "'Do Not Judge,'" 181.

Dominus Iesus begins by stating that the Church's mission, born from the Final Commandment (Mark 16: 15–16; Matt 28:18–20), is to proclaim the mystery of the triune God and the mystery of the incarnation of the Son as the saving event for all humanity (§1). But because that mission is still far from complete at the close of the second millennium and in view of interreligious dialogue—advanced by the Second Vatican Council—the Church's proclamation today has to also "make use of the practice of inter-religious dialogue" (§2). The thrust of the declaration is that "relativistic theories" are problematic as they hold that "certain truths have been superseded" (§4). Specifically, "relativistic theories which seek to justify religious pluralism, not only *de facto* but also *de jure (or in principle)*," endanger the "Church's constant missionary proclamation" (§4). It is in this context that the declaration seeks to establish the essential truth of "the definitive and complete character of the revelation of Jesus Christ." This "must be *firmly believed*," the declaration declares, just as the "proper response to God's revelation is '*the obedience of faith*' . . . by which man freely entrusts his entire self to God, offering 'the full submission of intellect and will to God who reveals' and freely assenting to the revelation given by him" (§7). The declaration then states that God also reveals through other religions, even as they may "contain 'gaps, insufficiencies and errors'" (§8).

"The Church's Magisterium," therefore, "reasserts that Jesus Christ is the mediator and the universal redeemer" (§11). In simple terms this assertion is that Jesus is not only the "one and only" savior but that he is at the same time also the savior "for all." Moreover, "just as there is one Christ, so there exists 'a single Catholic and apostolic Church.'" "This Church," the declaration clarifies, "subsists in [*subsistit in*] the Catholic Church, governed by the Successor of Peter and by the Bishops in communion with him" (§16). The declaration then pronounces that "the mission of the Church is 'to proclaim and establish among all peoples the kingdom of Christ and of God,' and that 'she is on earth, the seed and the beginning of the kingdom'" (§18). "At the same time," the declaration qualifies, "it rules out, in a radical way, that mentality of indifferentism 'characterized by a religious relativism which leads to the belief that one religion is as good as another'" (§22). Hence, "if it is true that the followers of other religions can receive divine grace, it is also certain that *objectively speaking* they are in a gravely deficient situation in comparison with those who, in the Church, have the fullness of the means of salvation" (§22). In interreligious dialogue, therefore, "the mission *ad gentes* 'today as always retains its full force and necessity'" (§22). Indeed, interreligious dialogue, as part of the Church's evangelizing mission, "is just one of the actions of the Church in her mission *ad gentes*" (§22). The Church, therefore, must continue to announce "the necessity of conversion to Jesus Christ and of adherence to the Church through Baptism, and the other sacraments, in order to participate fully in communion with God, the Father, Son and Holy Spirit" (§22).

REACTIONS TO DOMINUS IESUS

Since *Dominus Iesus* is a document that cautions against relativism, which is alleged to have been a consequence of interreligious dialogue, one would have expected the reactions from people of other religions to be vociferous. But, in reality, they were few and far between. One reason given is that people of other religions do not generally read Church documents. Moreover, Church documents seldom feature in interreligious discourse. The more important element in interreligious relations is the attitude of the actual dialogue partners. Usually these are Christians and persons of other religions who do not harbor exclusivist views, or else they would not be in the ministry of dialogue in the first place.

Arvind Sharma, an Indian Hindu teaching at McGill University, confirms this: "I've never met a Catholic who begins a dialogue from such a point of view,"[4] obviously referring to the sentiments expressed in *Dominus Iesus*. "If they did, what would we have to talk about?" he asks rhetorically. Rabbi Jonathan Romain of the United Kingdom reinforces the view: "The Catholic bishops with whom I've spoken all say they're extremely embarrassed, extremely sorry." He was referring to the reactions of some bishops to *Dominus Iesus*. Farid Esack, a Muslim scholar from South Africa, takes a self-critical look at his own religious community and suggests: "Many Muslims take exactly the same kind of position as the Vatican, that you have to stand under Islam in order to understand truth; that the only way to salvation is through normative Islam." Because he himself has been very much engaged in interreligious dialogue, he then asks, again rhetorically, "If that's how we feel, what can dialogue consist

---

4. Allen, "Gap between Theory," line 8. Subsequent quotes in this paragraph are from lines 19–50 of this source.

of? I give you a Qur'an. You give me a Bible and some papal documents. We have a cup of tea and that's it."

Other reactions, especially those from Asia, were much more pointed. C. S. Radhakrishnan, a Hindu from Goa, pointed out that the Vatican declaration would probably foster "unnecessary animosity and frivolous irritations."[5] Radhakrishnan then expressed surprise that the followers of a "merciful Christ" could espouse such "intolerant language." Shiekh Jamal, a Muslim journalist also of Goa, remarks that the *Dominus Iesus* declaration has a "language of antagonism," and therefore cannot be useful for dialogue. P. P. Shirodkar, the man who had requested Pope John Paul II to apologize for the Inquisition in the formerly Portuguese Goa during the pope's visit to India in 1999, suggests that the Vatican text was an example of the "external trapping of religion [that] is the villain dividing man and man." J. P. Singh, a Sikh by religion, believes that the document leaves "no room for other religions to exist." Such an attitude simply goes against the Sikh religious teachings, which are unambiguous in communicating that the various religions are alternative routes to God.

Indian media reports were no less critical. The *Organizer*, the mouthpiece of the Rashtriya Swayamsevak Sangh (National Volunteer Corps), which has links to the nationalist BJP political party of India, claimed that *Dominus Iesus* filled with "16th-century papal arrogance," is bound to create tension in pluralistic societies such as India.[6] Suggesting that *Dominus Iesus* goes against "the basic philosophy of the Indian constitution," which regards all religions to be equal, the *Organizer* called on the federal government to launch a protest on the Vatican document as it "may cause communal disturbance in the country."[7] Such a thought, coming from a country that has seen a rise in the number of anti-Christian violence perpetuated by religious fundamentalists, could certainly serve as a caution, if not a warning.

RESPONSE OF THE ASIAN CHURCH

In view of such negative reactions coming from people of other religions, Church leaders and theologians in Asia were quick to offer their own re-

---

5. "Indians Shocked," lines 29–30. Subsequent quotes in this paragraph are from lines 30–46 of this source.

6. "Media Say Document Threatens," line 6.

7. Ibid., lines 7–13.

sponses. If anything, these responses sought to distance the Church in Asia from the Vatican document. The Catholic Bishops' Conference of India's standing committee, for example, circulated a document aimed at "toning down" the Vatican declaration.[8] The introduction to the circular noted that *Dominus Iesus* was "hotly debated" in India. As implied earlier, some of these debates could have led to catastrophic consequences, especially given the Church's minority status in predominantly Hindu India. The bishops, therefore, thought it important that they explicitly affirm the importance of Indian Catholics to remain patriotic and ensure the preservation of the best of the local cultures and other religions, all of which, the circular asserts, God uses as instruments for salvation.

Fr. Saby Vempeny, a scholar of Islam, compares the declaration to the "fatwas" or religious edicts of the Taliban.[9] It is a fatwa specifically directed towards the Church in Asia since they are the ones most engaged in the activity of interreligious dialogue. Vempeny expresses fear that the document would be used by anti-Christian elements as proof that Christians are fundamentalist and so deserve to be curbed. Another priest, Fr. Thomas Kuriakose, the former secretary of the Jesuit secretariat for dialogue in South Asia, regrets that the declaration appears insulting to those engaged in the mission of dialogue. His appraisal is that the Vatican document seems to ignore the human and pastoral dimensions of interreligious dialogue, making it seem that its authors are simply "not living in dialogue."[10] The sentiment was echoed by another Jesuit, Fr. Sebastian Painadath, who suggests that "this document hasn't grown out of lived experience." Referring to *Dominus Iesus*' aloof and detached language, Painadath, who is founder-director of Sameeksha Ashram, a center for Asian spirituality in Kerala, said, "It is a Western 'desk experience.'"[11]

Fr. Bao Tinh Vuong Dinh Bich, a commentator on Church-society relations in Vietnam, intimates that *Dominus Iesus* could present cultural problems for Vietnamese Catholics. Proposing that respect for the other's culture is a basic value incumbent upon followers of Jesus of Nazareth, he then observes that even if Jesus was an Oriental "the magisterial apparatus of the Catholic Church is located in Rome and its personnel are almost

---

8. "Bishops Note Room," line 1.
9. "Some Regret Language," line 6.
10. Ibid., line 71.
11. "Kingdom Value Core," line 114.

exclusively Westerners."[12] Thus accounts for the lack of understanding on the part of the drafters of the document on issues of cultural sensitivities, especially those peculiar to Asia. "If the drafters of the Declaration *Dominus Iesus* had spent a few weeks in the Asian region where Catholics are mostly a minority, they would have realized the cultural stakes brought about by the magisterial document that was written for the sake of the Church," Fr. Bich remarked.[13]

Xavierian Fr. Franco Sottocornola, director of Tozai Shukyo Koryu, an interreligious center in Japan, which he cofounded with a Buddhist monk, resounds Bich's comments by suggesting that *Dominus Iesus* has an "Occidental" tone. The "Oriental way," he continues, is more concerned about developing "human relationship first as preparation for dialogue."[14] The importance of building relationships was similarly echoed in Indonesia at a seminar organized by the Widya Sasana School of Philosophy and Theology in Malang. Vincentian Fr. Petrus Maria Handoko suggests that it was probably a conservative theologian afraid that the Catholic Church was becoming too friendly with other religions who formulated *Dominus Iesus*.[15]

EVIDENCE OF RENEWALIST CURRENTS

One of the most critical and at the same time hopeful response came from Jesuit Fr. Aloysius Pieris of Sri Lanka. One of Asia's foremost thinkers, Pieris spoke on *Dominus Iesus* when presenting a talk at the Ecumenical Institute for Study and Dialogue in Colombo on September 30, 2000. In lieu of discussing the Vatican declaration he chose, instead, to discuss the background to how the Church operates and why a document such as *Dominus Iesus* was promulgated. Specifically, Pieris looks at the Vatican declaration in the context of the renewal of the Second Vatican Council and the concomitant "ecclesiastical politics" surrounding the council, which, he asserts, continues even until today.

Pieris begins by observing that the "dynamics of the movement and counter-movements" within the Church today has its roots in Vatican II. He then reminds that it was a renewal council and not so much a reform

12. "*Dominus Iesus* Brings Tension," line 20.
13. Ibid., line 83.
14. "Japanese Indifferent," line 32.
15. "Theology Institute Initiates Discussion" (*UCAN*), line 37.

council. A reform, Pieris suggests, is a "controlled and graduated process of change that keeps the institutional set-up of the church intact."[16] Reform is a top-down process or change that is evoked from the center and moves out towards the periphery. The center issues decrees or procedures and the local churches, or periphery, implements them. Change is smooth, predictable, and well managed in reform councils. The First Vatican Council and the Council of Trent were reform councils. Renewal, on the other hand, is a movement in the opposite direction: "It irrupts from below and works its way up to the top volcanically." Renewals are initiated mainly by those at the peripheries "where fresh and new ideas flow in more freely than in the Center of the establishment." Pieris elaborates: "Renewalist currents that begin to whirl in the margin of the church surge into centripetal waves that dash on the fortified ecclesiastical structures. The resistance at the Center is inevitable. Yet, there is a gradual transformation to which the Center has to yield."[17]

It is in the context of these center-periphery dynamics that Pieris suggests he was more or less expecting a document such as *Dominus Iesus*. The Vatican declaration, according to his theory, is but the center's response to the various "irruptions" happening at the peripheries. Irruptions are by no means gentle, pleasant, or welcome. If anything, they are chaotic, abrasive and unsettling. Fear, worry, and trembling amidst irruptions are anticipated and understandable responses. *Dominus Iesus* seems to reveal these latter responses. It betrays a sense that the center is wary of the irruption that goes by the name of religious pluralism. Where the irruptions are intense, the center's response is adamant, firm, and unyielding. That *Dominus Iesus* uses such strong language—"to be firmly believed," "definitive and complete," "contrary to the Church's faith," "required to profess," "full submission"—seems to suggest that the irruptions from the periphery must have been relatively strong.

One could even suggest that *Dominus Iesus* is but a verification of the irruptions coming from the periphery. The periphery in question here is Asia, since religious pluralism is an existential reality confronting the Church in Asia. The Vatican declaration is, therefore, an expression of the inevitable resistance to the renewalist currents coming from Asia. This, of course, is nothing more than an articulation of the dialectics of change.

---

16. Pieris, "Roman Catholic Perception," 215.
17. Ibid.

The fresh and new ideas whirling in from Asia are evoking a proportionate reaction from the Roman center.

According to Pieris's theory, the process will continue for a while until such a time the center is ready to yield. Viewed from this perspective, *Dominus Iesus* is a document that engenders hope: hope that the Vatican II renewal in the area of the Church's relation with other religions is slowly but surely being taken seriously. The most significant players in this can be found in the Church of Asia.

BEGINNINGS OF THE IRRUPTIONS

The Second Vatican Council was, from its very inception, something unusual and unwelcome by the Vatican's center. Between the announcement and the opening of the council on October 11, 1962, the preparatory work was done by Curia members of the Vatican, many of whom actually preferred not to have a universal council at that point in the Church's history. Because they saw it as their duty to protect the faith and safeguard the Christian tradition, they viewed an imminent council, at a time when the Church was relatively stable and uniform, with some sort of skepticism.

Four key moments at the council were crucial.[18] The first was Pope John XXIII's opening address, where he urged the council fathers to take a pastoral direction. The second was when the bishop-delegates refused to vote on the Curia's nominations for the working commissions, insisting, instead, for more time to get to know one another first. The third moment was the vigorous debate on the draft documents. The majority wanted the drafts reworked to befit the theme of renewal. At one point when a vote was taken, 60 percent of the bishops voted to have the document withdrawn. Though this was insufficient to remand the text, Pope John XXIII intervened and ordered that the text be thoroughly revised. The vote and the intervention of the pope represent the fourth key moment.

In any case, what eventually happened as a result of the deliberations and decisions of the council prompted Church historian John O'Malley to assert that "never before in the history of Catholicism have so many and such sudden changes been legislated and implemented which immediately touched the lives of the faithful, and never before had such a radical adjustment of viewpoint been required of them."[19] One of the most suc-

---

18. Komonchak, "Vatican Council II."
19. O'Malley, *Tradition and Transition*, 17.

cinct ways to summarize these changes and the vision of the council is by reference to the 1964 encyclical *Ecclesiam Suam*, issued by John XXIII's successor, Pope Paul VI. In *Ecclesiam Suam* (its English title is "Paths of the Church"), Paul VI discusses the ways in which the Church must carry out its mission in the contemporary world. The pope spells this out in all its aspects but it can aptly be captured with one word, namely, "dialogue." By "dialogue" Paul VI refers to the four categories or levels of dialogue that the Church should be engaged in: (i) dialogue with the world and cultures, (ii) dialogue with other religions, (iii) dialogue with other Christians, and (iv) dialogue within the Church.

With this new mission mandate it is not surprising that the post-Vatican II Church was almost unrecognizable. Imbued with the spirit of renewal, bishops all over the world implemented changes in their parishes and dioceses in order to bring the Church to be more in tune with the contemporary world. Curial officials bent on conserving the Church's tradition sought to return the Church to the pre-Vatican II era. Pope Paul VI had the unenviable task of ensuring a balance between going with the flow of this new spirit of renewal and maintaining the status quo. The former represented the aspiration of the majority of the world's bishops while the latter meant accommodating to the concerns and fears of the conservative minority. A creative tension ensued. One significant manifestation of this tension was the 1968 document *Humanae Vitae*.

Paul VI had appointed an international commission of sixty-nine members (consisting of cardinals, theologians, medical doctors, ethicists, lay people, married couples, etc.) to study the issue of artificial contraception. After intense study and discussion, the commission voted sixty-four to four (one member was absent) in favor of changing the traditional teaching, which forbade the use of all forms of contraceptives. Paul VI agonized over the vote for more than a year before reaffirming the traditional ban in his 1968 encyclical. The conservative minority had won the day but the tension was far from over. It continues until today and takes the form of the center-periphery dynamics Pieris speaks about. The tensions, in the form of irruptions from the periphery and the concomitant reactions from the center, are inevitable for the renewal advocated by Vatican II to materialize. The discussion that follows reflects on these center-periphery dynamics.

THE FIRST IRRUPTION: LIBERATION THEOLOGY

The first of the key center-periphery dynamics took the shape of the theological movement that surfaced in Latin America shortly after Vatican II and went by the name of "liberation theology." Representing both a social and theological movement, liberation theology was a late-1960s irruption from Latin America. It was in part the fruits of Vatican II's call for the Church to be in dialogue with the local culture. In the Latin American context this effectively meant the engagement of the Church with the massive poverty and oppression of the masses by the dictatorial regimes.

The Second Vatican Council's document *Gaudium et Spes*, or the "Pastoral Constitution on the Church in the Modern World," provided the necessary starting point for liberation theology: "The joys and the hopes, the griefs and the anxieties of the men of this age, especially those who are poor or in any way afflicted, these too are the joys and hopes, the griefs and anxieties of the followers of Christ" (§1). Specifically, *Gaudium et Spes* looked at the Church-world relationship; it promoted the social dimension of human existence and especially the effects of sin; it pledged the Church's commitment to the massive social problems confronting humanity; it recognized the insufficiency of individualist morality to apprehend social issues; it encouraged local Churches to explore the root causes of such problems, using tools from the social sciences if necessary; and it encouraged theologians to inculturate the Gospel in their own particular contexts.[20]

This mandate from Vatican II received its first "baptism" at the 1968 Second *Consejo Episcopal Latinoamericana* (CELAM), which met in Medellin, Colombia. Analyzing the situation of poverty and the injustice that prevailed in the Latin American continent, the Medellin conference not only endorsed the mandate of Vatican II but also committed the whole Church to the integral development and liberation of the people of the continent. This required a "preferential option for the poor." With the Medellin blessings, liberation theology developed rapidly, aided by a host of liberation theologians, among the more renowned being the Uruguayan Juan Luis Segundo, Peruvian Gustavo Gutierrez, Brazilian Leonardo Boff, and Basque Jon Sobrino, who had been working in El Salvador. It was Gutierrez's 1971 book, the English translation of which

---

20. Haight, "Liberation Theology," 570–76.

was entitled *A Theology of Liberation*, that "canonized" the label "liberation theology" and popularized the theology worldwide.

CENTER ENCOUNTERS LIBERATION THEOLOGY

In keeping with the dialectics-of-renewal theory, the advances made by liberation theology at the periphery were met with a sense of suspicion and apprehension at the center. Three events seem to betray this reactive sense. Firstly, as early as 1975 the Congregation for the Doctrine of the Faith opened a file on Leonardo Boff and, in 1980, on Jon Sobrino.[21] Secondly, a 1977 document of the International Theological Commission entitled "Human Development and Christian Salvation" spoke positively about liberation theology. To offer a balance the document also expressed a number of reservations and warnings about some possible pitfalls. Thirdly, when Pope John Paul II spoke to the bishops at the third CELAM in Puebla in 1979, conservative members of the conference wanted a condemnation of liberation theology and a reversal of the Medellin option. After intense deliberations, the bishops at Puebla continued to affirm the "option for the poor," but not without first issuing a variety of cautions. It was at best a compromise document.

With the ascendancy of John Paul II to the helm of the Church in 1978 and Joseph Ratzinger to the head of the CDF in 1981, the Roman Curia's suspicion over liberation theology intensified. Ratzinger's CDF had actually begun work on liberation theology earlier and formally came out in condemnation of it in the 1984 document *Libertatis Nuntius*, or "Instruction on Certain Aspects of the Theology of Liberation." This document essentially expanded on the 1977 document of the International Theological Commission, except that it focused principally on the latter's one-paragraph negative comments of liberation theology while significantly leaving out all the positive elements. The reaction to this 1984 document was dramatic, causing the pope to call for another study, resulting in a more positive document, which came out in 1986. This latter document, *Libertatis Conscientia*, or "Instruction on Christian Freedom and Liberation," afforded a more positive vision of liberation theology and was hailed as a vindication by the liberationists.

If there was any doubt about the CDF's interest in liberation theology, an address by then-Cardinal Ratzinger to the presidents of the

---

21. Allen, "Authentic Liberation," in Allen, *Cardinal Ratzinger*, 147–74.

Doctrinal Commission of CELAM, held in Mexico in May 1996, cleared such doubt. Ratzinger began his speech by saying that "in the '80s, the theology of liberation in its radical forms seemed to be the most urgent challenge for the faith of the church."[22] He then went on to assert that the fall of communism in Eastern Europe "turned out to be a kind of twilight of the gods for that theology of redeeming political praxis."[23] Through this statement Ratzinger was more or less expressing that the challenge posed by liberation theology had been successfully addressed and that it was no longer a problem. The center-periphery conflict had been assuaged; the irruptions no longer represented a serious threat. Liberation theology had moved out of the CDF's spotlight.

On the other hand, observers recount that what began at the periphery has already influenced the center. Themes advanced by liberation theologians have since been integrated into mainstream theology. For example, John Paul II's 1987 encyclical *Sollicitudo Rei Socialis*, "On Social Concerns," integrated so many of the concerns held by Leonardo Boff and others that a wishful number of people have suggested it could have been written by a liberation theologian. The Pontifical Biblical Commission's 1984 study of "The Bible and Christology" made reference to Boff, Gustavo Gutierrez, and Jon Sobrino, as well as to the theme of "Christ the liberator."[24] The same commission, in a 1993 study on "The Interpretation of the Bible in the Church," again discussed liberation theology, including the contextual liberationist approach to interpreting the Bible.[25] Thus, even if liberation theology has been curbed in some avenues at the periphery, it has more or less become incarnate at the center. This, according to Aloysius Pieris's theory, was inevitable as the center has little choice but to gradually yield to the renewalist currents of the periphery.

THE SECOND IRRUPTION:
THEOLOGY OF RELIGIOUS PLURALISM

If Ratzinger's 1996 Mexico address marked the end of the CDF's spotlight on Latin America, it also turned the spotlight in the direction of Asia. For, in that same address, Ratzinger remarked that "relativism has thus be-

22. Ratzinger, "Relativism," line 1.
23. Ibid., line 24.
24. Pontifical Biblical Commission, "Bible and Christology."
25. Pontifical Biblical Commission, "Interpretation of Bible."

come the central problem for the faith at the present time."[26] Elaborating further, Ratzinger said, "the so-called pluralist theology of religion has been developing progressively since the '50s. Nonetheless, only now has it come to the center of the Christian conscience." He continues: "On the one hand, relativism is a typical offshoot of the Western world and its forms of philosophical thought, . . . on the other it is connected with the philosophical and religious institutions of Asia especially, and surprisingly, with those of the Indian subcontinent." Attempting to associate these two systems, Ratzinger explains:

> The two philosophies are fundamentally different both for their departure point and for the orientation they imprint on human existence. Nonetheless, they seem to mutually confirm one another in their metaphysical and religious relativism. The religious and pragmatic relativism of Europe and America can get a kind of religious consecration from India which seems to give its renunciation of dogma the dignity of a greater respect before the mystery of God and of man. In turn, the support of European and American thought to the philosophical and theological vision of India reinforces the relativism of all the religious forms proper to the Indian heritage.

While the experience of religious pluralism and the theology propounded to address it seem to have come into the consciousness of the universal Church only in recent decades, it is not so for Christians living in Asia. One could even say that the phenomenon of religious pluralism has always been a part of the Asian Christian's psyche for as long as Christianity has been in that part of the world. It comes as no surprise then that Asian theologians have been at the forefront of constructing and developing Christian theologies to attend to the phenomenon of religious pluralism. They, in turn, have been the focal point of the Vatican's concern. The next chapter will explore this in greater detail, pointing to why the Vatican's *Dominus Iesus* is seen as having a direct bearing on the development of an Asian theology of religious pluralism.

---

26. Ratzinger, "Relativism," line 48. Subsequent quotes are from lines 76–87 and 138–46 of this source.

2

Religious Pluralism and Asian Theology[1]

LIKE LIBERATION THEOLOGY, THE theology of religious pluralism also has its official roots in Vatican II. It is the fruit of Vatican II's call for the Church to be in dialogue with other religions. If liberation theology takes as starting point *Gaudium et Spes*, the theology of religious pluralism takes as starting point *Nostra Aetate*, the "Declaration on the Relationship of the Church to Non-Christian Religions," issued in 1965. Though a very short document, with merely five articles, it has significantly transformed the manner in which the Church relates with people of other religions. In particular, the following article was revolutionary, at least by the ecclesia standards of the 1960s:

> The Catholic Church rejects nothing which is true and holy in these religions. She looks with sincere respect upon those ways of conduct and of life, those rules and teachings which, though differing in many particulars from what she holds and sets forth, nevertheless often reflect a ray of that Truth which enlightens all men. (§2)

THEOLOGY OF RELIGIONS

While it was Vatican II that officially "canonized" the exploration of the Church's relation with other religions, efforts had already begun in the years preceding the Council. To be sure, the 1950s and the years leading up to the Council witnessed a change in the Church's attitude towards other religions. It went from an attitude that was predominantly apologetic and negative to one that was less defensive and tending towards the

---

1. A significant portion of this chapter was published as "*Dominus Iesus* and Asian Theologies" in *Horizons* 29 (Fall 2002) 278–89.

positive. This was about the time when the exploration was mainly in the realm of what is known as the "theology of religion." This theology asks "what religion is and seeks, in the light of Christian faith, to interpret the universal religious experience of humankind; it further studies the relationship between revelation and faith, faith and religion, and faith and salvation."[2]

In exploring religious experience, the "theology of religion" developed into what is known as the "theology of religions." This latter theology takes the exploration a little further to focus on "the various [religious] traditions in the context of the history of salvation and in their relationship to the mystery of Jesus Christ and the Christian Church."[3] The other religions are now explored to discern their role in the salvation of their members and affirmed for the positive values they contain. In this regard, *Nostra Aetate* represents the Church's official affirmation of the theology of religions. This represented the dominant focus of the Church of the Second Vatican Council, where theology confined itself to exploring the role of other religions in the economy of God's salvation.

The 1980s saw the development of broader perspectives in the Church's theology of other religions:

> Going beyond the problematic of people's salvation in and through their religious traditions, the new perspective seeks to penetrate more deeply into God's plan for humankind. It asks about the significance of the plurality of religious traditions in that plan—and consequently in the unfolding of the history of God's dealings with humankind which we call the history of salvation.[4]

Thus began in a more systematic manner what has come to be known as the "theology of religious pluralism." This theology is different from its predecessor in that it no longer asks about the possibility of salvation for persons of other religions; it presumes that. It also no longer preoccupies itself with the exploration of the role the other religions play in salvation; that, too, is presumed. Instead, "it seeks more deeply, in the light of Christian faith, for the meaning in God's design for humankind of the plurality of living faiths and religious traditions with which we are surrounded. Are all the religious traditions of the world destined, in God's

2. Dupuis, *Toward a Theology of Pluralism*, 7.
3. Ibid., 8.
4. Ibid., 13.

plan, to converge? Where, when, and how?" In other words, religious pluralism is considered not so much "as a matter of course and a fact of history (pluralism *de facto*) but as having a raison d'être in its own right (pluralism *de jure*)."[5]

THE "PROBLEM" OF ASIAN THEOLOGY

While it was individual theologians—of Asia as well as of the West—who were most responsible for the development of the theology of religious pluralism, the Federation of Asian Bishops' Conferences (FABC) also played a significant role. In particular, at the very first FABC Plenary Assembly in 1974, in discussing the theme of "Evangelization in Modern Day Asia," the bishops defined the task of evangelization in Asia as follows:

> In Asia especially this involves a dialogue with the great religious traditions of our peoples. In this dialogue we accept them as significant and positive elements in the economy of God's design of salvation. In them we recognize and respect profound spiritual and ethical meanings and values. Over many centuries they have been the treasury of the religious experience of our ancestors, from which our contemporaries do not cease to draw light and strength. They have been (and continue to be) the authentic expression of the noblest longings of their hearts, and the home of their contemplation and prayer. They have helped to give shape to the histories and cultures of our nations. (§14)[6]

The bishops then reveal their own position on this by asking rhetorically, "How then can we not give them reverence and honor? And how can we not acknowledge that God has drawn our peoples to Himself through them?" (§15). This 1974 statement, together with the many subsequent statements of the FABC, provided the necessary endorsement by the magisterium of the Church in Asia to Asian theologians as they went about their reflections on the theology of religious pluralism. That support notwithstanding (or could it be precisely because of this official endorsement?), a number of Asian theologians have since come under the scrutiny of Vatican Curial officials, in particular the Congregation for the Doctrine of the Faith.

---

5. Ibid., 10–11.
6. Rosales and Arevalo, *All Peoples of Asia*, 1:14.

If the Roman center's interest in theologies of religious pluralism was officially inaugurated by then-Cardinal Ratzinger's 1996 speech in Mexico, hints of such an interest had already been given over the years. Among the first such hints came in a statement made by Cardinal Josef Tomko, the prefect of the Congregation for the Evangelization of Peoples. In a 1991 address to his fellow cardinals, Tomko hinted that interreligious dialogue seemed to be leading towards "doctrinal confusion" and that "although India is the epicenter to this tendency and Asia is its principal camp, . . . these ideas already circulate in Oceania, in some African countries and in Europe."[7] The focus on India as the "epicenter" was subsequently repeated by other Curial officials. Ratzinger himself, in an address to the presidents of the FABC member conferences and episcopal chairpersons of doctrinal commissions, also explicitly mentioned India: "The problem which arises in India, but also elsewhere, comes to expression in [Raimon] Panikkar's famous phrase: 'Jesus is Christ, but Christ is not (only) Jesus.'"[8]

Thus, when the Vatican declaration *Dominus Iesus* was issued it came as no surprise that many suspected the targets were the theologians from Asia in general and India in particular. Aside from Ratzinger's specific mention of the "negative theology of Asia" in his introductory comments, a statement by Cardinal Edward Cassidy, then-president of the Pontifical Council for Promoting Christian Unity, was also revealing. Cassidy, in appealing to Jewish leaders who had decided to boycott a Judeo-Christian function on account of the insensitive posture taken by *Dominus Iesus*, tries to explain: "The text is not directed to the ecumenical and interreligious realm, but to the academic world." Cassidy then hit the nail on the head when he continued: "Above all, it was directed to theology professors of India, because in Asia there is a theological problem over the oneness of salvation."[9]

While it is perceived that *Dominus Iesus* was directed at Asia, its principal targets were actually the theologians of religious pluralism. These may be Asians, but not necessarily so. For example, the American Paul Knitter and the Brit John Hick were severely criticized by Ratzinger in his 1996 speech in Mexico. In fact, Ratzinger based almost his entire critique

7. Tomko, "Proclaiming Christ," 4.
8. Ratzinger, "Christ, Faith, Challenge," line 580.
9. "Cassidy Appeals," lines 19–23.

of the theology of religious pluralism on the works of these two scholars. Hick is a Presbyterian and Knitter, though criticized and probably investigated at lower levels, have never been officially censured. Others, however, were not as fortunate. For example, the German theologian Perry Schmidt-Leukel lost a professorship position at the University of Munich because he could not obtain the *nihil obstat* from his local archbishop, supposedly upon the advice of Ratzinger.[10] Ratzinger had made reference to Schmidt-Leukel's book *Theology of Religions* in his 1996 address at Mexico, indicating his familiarity with the latter's works. American Jesuit Roger Haight was barred from teaching at Boston's Weston School of Theology while the CDF launched an inquiry into his book *Jesus, Symbol of God*. Haight's interpretation of the mystery of the Trinity, Christ's divinity, and the role of Jesus in salvation were aspects under investigation.

As can be seen from the preceding discussion, the common denominator for the theologians mentioned above is that their theology has to do with the issues raised by the phenomenon of religious pluralism. While they may be scholars from the West, most have had very direct experiences in Asia or are involved in interreligious dialogue in their own way. Scholars from the East (read: Asia) have not been spared by the Vatican's scrutiny either. They have, in fact, had a much more difficult time as compared to their Western counterparts.

ASIAN THEOLOGIANS OF RELIGIOUS PLURALISM

As alluded to earlier, the Roman center's interest in theologies of religious pluralism is but a reaction to the irruptions coming from the periphery. The periphery of interest here is Asia, and the subjects in question are its theologians. To be sure, numerous Asian theologians have files with the CDF; some have been investigated at local levels while others have experienced direct Vatican interference in their appointments to head particular theological institutions.

In the mid-1990s a group of Indian bishops were summoned by the CDF for a seminar or "dialogue session," as it was called, during which the works of their theologians were discussed. Later, the editors of *Vidyajyoti*, a reputable theological journal in India, received a letter from the CDF raising questions about the theological orientations of some of the jour-

---

10. Allen, *Cardinal Ratzinger*, 242–44.

nal's contributors. Suffice to say that the CDF has pursued quite a few of these cases in Asia.

Of these, three stand out as most significant for the Church in Asia. The first is the case of Tissa Balasuriya, who, after a scrutiny lasting several years, was excommunicated, only to be reinstated upon intense protests from many quarters both of people inside as well as outside of the Church. The second case is that of Anthony De Mello, whose works were condemned posthumously. Because the dead cannot defend themselves he remains castigated, but not without his superiors in India coming to his defense first. The third case, which is of the most significance to *Dominus Iesus*, is that of Jacques Dupuis, a Belgian Jesuit who had served more than three decades in India. A respected scholar and very much identified with Indian and Asian theology, Dupuis's investigation came as a surprise to many since he had always been regarded as mainstream and cautious in his theologizing. If not for the insistent defense put up by Dupuis and his superiors he would have been regarded as having committed serious theological errors. Though ultimately vindicated, he still had to admit to the possibility of leading others to error. In view of the relevance and significance of these three cases to our discussion, especially in understanding the concerns raised by *Dominus Iesus*, they shall be looked at in greater detail.

The Case of Tissa Balasuriya

A priest of the Oblates of Mary Immaculate (OMI) order, Fr. Tissa Balasuriya is the founder-director of the Center for Society and Religion located in Colombo, Sri Lanka. In that capacity he published, in a double issue of the Center's regular journal, *Logos*, a 192-page book entitled *Mary and Human Liberation*, in 1990. A few bishops from the Sri Lankan hierarchy were not happy with the publication and therefore appointed an *ad hoc* theological commission to review the book as early as mid-1992. Subsequently, in June 1994, the Catholic Bishops' Conference of Sri Lanka issued a statement to warn against the book's content, citing incompatibility with "the faith of the Church regarding the doctrine of revelation and its transmission, Christology, soteriology and Mariology."[11]

---

11. CDF, "Notification Concerning Balasuriya," lines 2–3. The next two quotes are from lines 12 and 16 of this source.

The following month, in July 1994, the CDF sent eleven pages of "observations on the text" to the OMI superior general, asking the latter to "take the measures appropriate in such a case." The letter was forwarded to Balasuriya for his response. In a series of unpublished letters to friends and supporters Balasuriya cited fifty-eight counts of unproved generalization, misunderstandings, misinterpretations, and falsifications of his text. In November 1995, the CDF proposed that Balasuriya sign a specially prepared Profession of Faith "to assist the author to demonstrate his full and unconditioned adherence to the Magisterium." According to the letters that Balasuriya sent out, included in this special Profession of Faith are two particular articles towards the end. The first one insists that Balasuriya accepts and holds that the Church has no authority whatsoever to confer priestly ordination on women, while the other advices that he adheres with religious submission to the teachings which either the Roman pontiff or the college of bishops enunciate when they exercise the authentic Magisterium even if they proclaim those teachings in an act that is not definitive.

Balasuriya responded to the notification by signing, instead, Pope Paul VI's 1968 solemn profession of faith, *Solemni Hac Liturgia* (or "Credo of the People of God"), with a caveat that he was signing it "in the context of theological development and Church practice since Vatican II and the freedom and responsibility of Christians and theological searchers, under Canon Law."[12] The CDF found the appended clause sufficient grounds to render the Profession of Faith "defective, since it diminished the universal and permanent value of the definitions of the Magisterium."[13] Hence, on January 2, 1997, an official notification was issued and, invoking Canon 1364 §1, declared that Balasuriya had incurred excommunication *latae sententiae*, or automatic excommunication, a sentence reserved for apostates, heretics, and schismatics. On account of the reactions and protests from all over the world, the CDF rescinded the excommunication a year later and Balasuriya was formally reconciled with the Church on January 15, 1998.

While it was what he said—or rather, what he wrote—that got Balasuriya into the quandary with the CDF, it was how the latter responded—or the manner in which it acted—that drew the most criticisms. In

12. Evers, "Excommunication," 213–14.
13. CDF, "Notification Concerning Balasuriya," line 28.

particular, the following issues drew condemnation: lack of due process; unwillingness on the part of the Sri Lankan Church's hierarchy and the CDF to discuss his views openly; presumption of guilt; the secret trial where the prosecutor is also the judge; and the harshness of the penalty.

The secular media, for example, *Time* and *Asiaweek* magazines, had a field day reporting on the injustice of the Church to one of its own. The Vatican was warned that the Church would lose all credibility to speak on behalf of justice unless the excommunication was rescinded. Leaders of the Sri Lankan Oblates urged that the penalty be repealed. Theologians of the Ecumenical Association of Third World Theologians (EATWOT) declared they would continue to regard Balasuriya as a theologian and priest despite the excommunication. The Hong Kong-based Asian Human Rights Association launched a fierce campaign of protest against the Vatican. In Aachen, Germany, the Institute of Missiology Missio lamented the "disturbing indication of a more fundamental problem of malfunction of theological communication within the Catholic Church." The Missio's statement then went on to say that "there has been an opposite trend as well which sees in the development of new contextual theologies not so much as enrichment but a threat against the unity of faith and doctrine in the Church."[14]

As is clear, the Balasuriya case was but an example of the tension between the Roman center and the Asian periphery. Bearing in mind that the excommunication came within months of Ratzinger's 1996 speech in Mexico, the matter is viewed as not so much an isolated event but as one within the larger context of "irruptions" and "reactions." Jesuit theologian Gispert-Sauch of India concludes that the Balasuriya case "certainly comes within a history of a tension between a centralized exercise of authority in the Church and the desires of many churches, not only in the Third World, to have more autonomy for their local communities."[15]

Even if the Balasuriya case highlighted the issue of judicial process within the Church, the theological issues that, in the first place, caused the whole episode can by no means be ignored. In his excommunication, coming as it did within months of Ratzinger's "Relativism" speech, it is not surprising that "relativism" was the central critique by the CDF of Balasuriya's *Mary and Human Liberation*. The notification alleges that "Fr.

---

14. "Statement by Missio," 120–21.
15. Gispert-Sauch, "Reflections around Balasuriya Case," 122.

Balasuriya does not recognize the supernatural, unique and irrepeatable character of the revelation of Jesus Christ, by placing its presuppositions on the same level as those of other religions."[16] He is accused of denying "the nature of Catholic dogma" and charged with "relativizing the revealed truths contained in them." The notification specifically alleges that "the author relativizes Christological dogma" and imputes that Balasuriya speaks of Jesus in terms "whose divine sonship is never explicitly recognized . . . and whose salvific function is only doubtfully acknowledged." It also charged that "Fr. Balasuriya reduces salvation . . . and so denies the necessity of Baptism." Balasuriya's Mariology was also scrutinized and, in this regard, the CDF alleges that "a fundamental aspect of the thought of Fr. Balasuriya is the denial of the dogma of original sin" and that "the author arrives at the point of denying in particular, the Marian dogmas."

On his part, Balasuriya denied all the charges and appealed, instead, for dialogue. In view of the numerous protests and the pressures that came from various quarters within the Church's hierarchy itself, dialogue was facilitated. A year later the CDF revoked the excommunication and Balasuriya was reconciled on the basis of a "decent and honorable" agreement.[17] Later, Balasuriya informed that the agreed-upon Statement of Reconciliation" that he signed contained the affirmation that "doctrinal errors were perceived in my writing and therefore provoked negative reactions from other parties, [which also] affected relationships and led to [the] unfortunate polarization in the ecclesial community. I truly regret the harm this caused."[18]

In effect, what Balasuriya regretted was not so much any theological error on his part but rather the harm caused by the perceptions of errors and the negative reactions. That the CDF yielded to his signing the 1968 Profession of Faith instead of the specially prepared one meant, according to Balasuriya, "*de facto*, an acceptance that no error had been proved in my book." The book remains in circulation and has, in fact, been republished several times since!

---

16. CDF, "Notification Concerning Balasuriya," line 91. The subsequent quotes are from lines 103–21 of this source.

17. Schaeffer, "Condemned Priest Restored," line 9.

18. Balasuriya, "Thank You," 250.

The Case of Anthony De Mello

Another Asian who caught the attention of the Vatican on account of his books is Fr. Anthony De Mello. An Indian Jesuit who died at the young age of fifty-six in 1987, De Mello had his books investigated posthumously, more than ten years after his death. He was the founder-director of the Sadhana Institute of Pastoral Counseling in Lonavla, India. A counselor and theologian, De Mello was well known as a spiritual writer and retreat master, not only in India but throughout the English-speaking world as well.

The Indian bishops noted that "his books have been published in dozens of languages in several continents and still today are read by not only Catholic priests and laity but by a wide range of educated followers of other religious traditions and secular ideologies."[19] Doubleday, the largest publisher of De Mello's books in the United States, informed that they used to carry eight De Mello titles in print and had sales running into "the millions."[20]

While De Mello's books were certainly much loved by many, they were also viewed with suspicion by some. Some Western right-wing Catholic papers, for instance, launched an attack on his books. In response, the Jesuit provincials for South Asia sought help from Jesuits around the world to come to the dead priest's defense. The incident resulted in the Vatican's interest in De Mello's works. Consequently, in June 1998, the CDF issued a notification "in order to protect the good of the Christian faithful" as they had found that De Mello's theological positions "are incompatible with the Catholic faith and can cause grave harm."[21] In the Explanatory Note that accompanied the notification, the CDF introduces De Mello's works as almost always taking "the form of short anecdotes presented in an accessible and easy-to-read style." It acknowledges that De Mello's earlier works, "while revealing the influence of Buddhist and Taoist spiritual currents, . . . remained in many respects within the boundaries of Christian spirituality." Nevertheless, even in these earlier works "and to a greater degree in his later publications, one notices a progressive distancing from the essential contents of the Christian faith."

---

19. Standing Committee, "Pastoral Guidelines de Mello," 606.

20. Allen, "De Mello Censure," line 68.

21. CDF, "Notification Concerning De Mello," lines 47–48. The subsequent quotes are from lines 60, 9, 14, and 308 of this source.

"For this reason," the explanatory note concludes, "those responsible for safeguarding the doctrine of the faith have been obliged to illustrate the dangers in the texts written by Father Anthony De Mello or attributed to him, and to warn the faithful about them."

In their first biannual meeting after the De Mello notification the Jesuit provincials of South Asia issued a statement voicing their concern over the Vatican's mistrust of Asian theology in general and the works of Jesuits such as Anthony De Mello and Jacques Dupuis in particular. Testifying to De Mello's effectiveness, they asserted that his books have helped many in Asia "in gaining freedom and in deepening their life of prayer."[22] The provincials invited the Vatican to support the pioneering works of theologians "with trust that is sympathetic but not naive, critical but not censorious." A few months later, in mid-1999, the bishops of India, through the Standing Committee of the Catholic Bishops' Conference of India, issued a statement entitled "Pastoral Guidelines on the Writings of Late Fr. Tony De Mello."

The statement begins by acknowledging the "authentic potential for good from Fr. Tony's publications" and goes on to recount the testimony of those who "knew him and heard him with profit especially when he preached a retreat to the Bishops of India." It then informs that the "Bishops of India read Fr. Tony's words and interpret his writings in [the] context of the very complex Indian religio-cultural situation from which Fr. Tony wrote and spoke." The bishops' statement also makes mention of "India's religio-cultural history over the past fifty years in which fanatical religious fundamentalism and communalism have caused hundreds of thousands of killings in God's name." In such a context "texts of scriptures and popular traditions have been twisted . . . so as to legitimize such human rights' violations as untouchability, child marriages, exorbitant dowries and so-called self-immolations of widows and new brides." De Mello's aim was "to facilitate an awakening so that persons could live more authentically with the inner freedom of God's children as promised them by the Gospel." The statement clarifies that De Mello "was not writing books of theology." He used the "medium of story-telling, . . . an eastern tradition of imparting wisdom," even if at times this may seem inadequate, especially "when it comes to precision of thought and clarity of expression." The bishops acknowledge that De Mello's "understanding

---

22. "Provincials Decry," line 23.

of divine revelation as mainly new awareness and consciousness is admittedly weak when measured up against a clear fidelity to the teaching of the Church." They then went on to clarify the seven principal themes that the notification points to as weaknesses in De Mello's works.

First, the notification takes issue with De Mello's portrayal of the revelation of God in Jesus as "an intuition of God without form or image, to the point of speaking of God as pure void." The Indian bishops' advice was that "those who come across such statements should keep in mind the clear teaching of the Church on the objective truth regarding God, revealed in Christ." Second, the CDF's explanatory note accuses De Mello of tending towards relativism, especially with regard to Christian revelation. In response the Indian bishops suggested that these writings "must be understood in the context of a dialogical approach in our meeting with people in pluri-religious contexts." "However," the bishops were quick to add, "we Christians are expected to hold firmly to the uniqueness of Christian revelation in such dialogical contexts." Third, the explanatory note objects to De Mello's "unilateral and exaggerated apophaticism." The notification describes it as a "radical apophaticism [which] leads even to a denial that the Bible contains valid statements about God." In response the Indian bishops' "Pastoral Guidelines" distinguish between "good apophatic language and very orthodox Catholicism" and "radical apophaticism." Acknowledging that "some of the writings of Fr. Tony [may] seem [like] apophatic statements which," the bishops agree, "go against the genuine and legitimate apophatic statements in the Christian tradition," they simply advise that "the readers of Fr. Tony De Mello should keep this in mind when they come across such statements in his writings." Fourth, the notification observes that De Mello "considers Jesus as a master alongside others," and that "Jesus is not recognized as the Son of God." The Indian bishops' response is that while we should "never compromise our faith in the divine sonship of Jesus," we should also look at De Mello's assertions "in the context of his readership—believers of every color of the rainbow and unbelievers, agnostics, atheists, humanists." Fifth, the notification posits that "the author's statement on the final destiny of man give rise to perplexity." "At one point," it elaborates, "he speaks of a 'dissolving' into the impersonal God, as salt dissolves in water." In response the bishops of India acknowledge that "the metaphor of dissolving into God as salt dissolves into water is surely poor and could be misleading."

The bishops' "Guidelines" then affirm that "we Christians believe in an eternal destiny consisting of a personal communion with God." Sixth, the CDF worries that De Mello reduces experience to mere subjective imagination. The bishops of India caution that the "declaration of the ineffable character of reality should not imply any denial of objective reality independent of experience as awareness." Seventh, the notification takes exception with the fact that in De Mello's books "institutions of the Church are criticized indiscriminately." Reference is made to Sacred Scriptures and the Creed. In response the Indian bishops suggest that even as "fundamentalist attitude towards the interpretation of the Bible" are prevalent, "in opposing these attitudes we cannot reduce the Bible to mere sign posts given by God."

The "Pastoral Guidelines" of the Indian bishops concludes by expressing their gratefulness to the Holy See for "bringing certain unacceptable formulation in the writings of [the] late Fr. Tony De Mello to our notice." They urged the faithful "to use a sense of balance and maintain a critical attitude as they read the books of Fr. Tony." Finally, unlike the CDF's notification, which ends by "warning the faithful" about the "dangers in the texts written by Father Anthony De Mello," the Indian bishops end by reasserting "the good these writings have done to many readers, both Christians and others."

The Case of Jacques Dupuis

The third case illustrating the center-periphery dynamics that indirectly gave rise to the Vatican declaration *Dominus Iesus* is that of Jacques Dupuis. A Belgian who went to India in 1948 to join the Jesuit scholasticate, Dupuis was to remain in India until 1984, during which time he taught Christology in various universities and seminaries.[23] It was there that he copublished—with another leading missionary theologian to India, Austrian Josef Neuner—the bestseller book *The Christian Faith in the Doctrinal Documents of the Catholic Church*. From 1984 Dupuis lived in Europe, where he taught at the Gregorian University in Rome. It was there that he researched on and wrote the book *Toward a Christian Theology of Religious Pluralism*, which saw its first publication in September 1997.

---

23. "Justice Denied." Subsequent quotes in the next paragraphs are from this source.

Within months, in June 1998, the CDF initiated a process against the book. Dupuis was informed of this at the end of September 1998, through his superior general, to whom all communications of the CDF were directed. He was given ten pages of questions, was told he had three months to respond to them, and that all of this was to be done in the strictest secrecy. Dupuis was allowed to consult only one theologian and this person had to be approved by his superior general. Meantime, he was forbidden to "spread his ideas," resulting in the cancellation of his course at Gregorian University, which in turn resulted in the investigation being made public.

On Christmas Day of 1998 Dupuis responded to the ten pages of questions by a written reflection of 188 pages, clarifying points that he felt had been misunderstood in his book. He waited until July 1999 before he received a response to his reflection. The response, which came from then-Cardinal Ratzinger (prefect of the CDF) through the Jesuit superior general, simply stated that his 188 pages were "unsatisfactory." He was again given yet another ten pages of questions and another three months to respond. Dupuis promptly responded and on November 1, 1999, sent in another sixty pages of answers to the queries. He then waited and waited, for ten long and agonizing months, during which time he was forbidden to discuss the investigation with anyone else save his superior general, Fr. Peter-Hans Kolvenbach, and his theological consultant, renowned Australian theologian Fr. Gerald O'Collins, also teaching at Gregorian.

Finally, on 1 September 1, 2000, Dupuis received an advanced copy of *Dominus Iesus* and a fifteen-page draft of a notification concerning his book. Together with Superior General Kolvenbach and O'Collins, Dupuis was granted a face-to-face meeting on September 4, 2000, with the CDF staff, namely, Cardinal Ratzinger, Archbishop Tarcisio Bertone, and Fr. Angelo Amato. He was instructed to sign the notification, which charged that his book contained "serious errors" against the faith, to which O'Collins asked where in Dupuis's book are the errors found. Ratzinger was taken aback when he realized that the imputed errors were really ideas from reviews others had made on Dupuis's book rather than Dupuis's own ideas found in his book. That the notification had no citation from Dupuis's book made it easy for them to verify that they were interpretations others had about his writings rather than Dupuis's own ideas. Nevertheless, Ratzinger then asked Dupuis to at least sign a statement that his book "was to be interpreted in the light of the Declaration

Dominus Iesus." Dupuis responded, "Your Eminence, you are asking too much of me." The meeting ended without any resolution.

The following day, September 5, *Dominus Iesus* was released. Dupuis's notification, had he signed it, would have been released two days later as some sort of sequel to *Dominus Iesus.* But because things did not work out as planned, Dupuis had another wait, and only three months later, on December 6, 2000, he received a new version of the notification. However, this time he was only asked to "Please sign." There would be no further discussion or alteration of the text whatsoever. Because signing meant an end to his ban on teaching or speaking about the case, he yielded and signed. Besides, the new version of the notification merely charged that his book contains "notable ambiguities and difficulties on important doctrinal points, which could lead a reader to erroneous or harmful opinions."

Interestingly, Dupuis points out that when the notification was eventually published more than a month later, on January 26, 2001, he was shocked when he discovered that an additional paragraph had been inserted into the text he had signed. This additional paragraph reads: "By signing the text, the author committed himself to assent to the stated theses and, in his future theological activity and publications, to hold the doctrinal contents indicated in the *Notification*, the text of which must be included in any reprinting or further editions of his book, as well as in all translations." Dupuis decided not to challenge it as he was now allowed to go on with his life and more importantly, to speak about the "shock and trauma" that he underwent for more than two years.

What precisely were the CDF's concerns about Dupuis's works? In Dupuis's own words, the first notification specifically mentions "serious errors against essential elements of Divine and Catholic faith," especially in the areas of "the doctrines on Incarnation, Trinity, Revelation." This, as mentioned earlier, was later amended to "ambiguities and difficulties" concerning the "interpretation of the sole and universal salvific mediation of Christ, the unicity and completeness of Christ's revelation, the universal salvific action of the Holy Spirit, the orientation of all people to the Church, and the value and significance of the salvific function of other religions." More importantly, Dupuis, who felt he was very much "identified with Asian thinking, especially with Indian theology," suspects that in his investigation the CDF's concerns were much more general. He sensed that it was the Asian theologians in general who were the primary concern and his investigation was but a message that they should "stop spreading such ideas that salvation is possible through other religions, or that the other religions can also be recipients of revelation, etc."

As one will notice readily, the themes explicitly expressed in Dupuis's notification are the very same themes that *Dominus Iesus* expounds upon. In fact, every one of the five themes in Dupuis's notification finds a correspondence in the six main headings or topics of *Dominus Iesus*. The first theme in Dupuis's notification, "On the sole and universal salvific mediation of Jesus Christ," corresponds to *Dominus Iesus*' third topic, "Unicity and universality of the salvific mystery of Jesus Christ." The second in Dupuis's, "On the unicity and completeness of revelation of Jesus Christ," corresponds to *Dominus Iesus*'s first topic, "The fullness and definitiveness of the revelation of Jesus Christ." Dupuis's third theme, "On the salvific action of the Holy Spirit," corresponds to part of *Dominus Iesus*'s second topic, "The Incarnate Logos and the Holy Spirit in the work of salvation." The fourth in Dupuis's case, "On the orientation of all human beings to the Church," corresponds to part of *Dominus Iesus*'s fourth topic, "The Church and the other religions in relation to salvation." The fifth and last theme found in the notification, "On the value and salvific function of the religious traditions," also constitutes part of *Dominus Iesus*'s fourth topic.

It is therefore clear that the various issues addressed by *Dominus Iesus* were the very same ones addressed by the notification issued on Jacques Dupuis. Additionally, of the seventeen footnotes in the notification, eleven of them have a citation taken from *Dominus Iesus*. It is therefore certainly not an exaggeration to suggest that Dupuis's notification was really a sequel to *Dominus Iesus*. They are both intimately related and mutually complementary. In this regard one can further understand why Ratzinger tried to insist, on September 4, 2000, that Dupuis signs the statement that his book "was to be interpreted in the light of the Declaration *Dominus Iesus*."

CENTER-PERIPHERY DYNAMICS IN ASIA

More importantly, it appears that one cannot but come to the conclusion that the various investigations into the works of Asian theologians were probably related to or could have led to the proclamation of the Vatican declaration *Dominus Iesus*. The declaration did not seem to have been an isolated document but had all the indications of an overall campaign undertaken by the Roman center in response to the disconcerting irruptions happening in Asia. These irruptions from the periphery go by the name "theology of religious pluralism." Hence, might it not be feasible to conclude that *Dominus Iesus* was promulgated specifically for the Church in Asia?

The declaration singles out the dangerous influence from what it alleges are "relativistic" theories advanced to address the phenomenon of religious pluralism. It regards the theologies of religious pluralism, which have arisen in the context of interreligious dialogue, as bordering upon relativism. To counter them, *Dominus Iesus* reaffirms the doctrines of the uniqueness and universality of Jesus Christ and of the Church and asserts that they must be upheld in the Church's dialogue with other religions. This, from the Asian side, is something that seems out of place and perhaps a bit too much to ask, unless a nuance is included that clearly indicates that they are not meant as denunciations of other religions. Otherwise, not only will the assertions of the uniqueness and universality of Christ and the Church be perceived as parochial and arrogant, it might even be construed as a neocolonial approach to interreligious relations. It does not help that people of other religions are already burdened with the memory of the history of colonial domination in which the Church is seen as an active accomplice. Thus, it looks like while Asian Christians have serious problems accepting the injunctions of *Dominus Iesus*, the Vatican magisterium expects nothing short of complete obedience in faith.

To be sure, as we saw in the last chapter, the reaction from Asian Christians, including members of the Asian Magisterium, was by and large negative when the declaration was promulgated. This was largely due to the perception that the document was out of sync with the realities of Christians living in multireligious contexts. It presents a thesis that more or less forces Asian Christians to be confronted with the choice of intellectually assenting to the Church's traditional teaching or appreciating their heart's calling to be open to other religions. It is as if they have to choose between accepting the doctrine of Christianity as the only true religion, on the one hand, and their lived reality on the other hand, which points to other religions as somewhat true in their own ways. It has to be pointed out here that many of these Asian Christians probably have friends, relatives, and family members who adhere to religions other than Christianity. For them, the theology of religious pluralism is by no means a metaphysical and abstract theological postulate, but an existential reality that impacts their family relations and dynamics.

This is why some scholars suggest that the drafters of *Dominus Iesus* are unable to appreciate the delicate circumstances in which Asian Christians relate to people of other religions—precisely because they do not have direct experience of dealing with the same. It is easy enough to assert the truth of one's own while at the same time diminishing those of others if one's horizon is basically limited to one's own religion. Perhaps Max Mueller's oft-cited dictum, "He who knows one knows none," is instructive for reflecting upon interreligious relations here. Unless one has knowledge of or experience of the *other*, it is not only difficult but also dangerous to be postulating any form of evaluation of or comparison between religions.

In the absence of such knowledge or experience on the part of the Curial officials responsible for *Dominus Iesus*, it comes as no surprise that they insist on total submission to the time-tested truths of the Christian tradition. In a way, this tension between the Vatican Magisterium and the Asian Church can also be seen as a choice between giving significance and priority to the place of *tradition* or that of *experience* in one's theological reflection. It is a methodological concern and reveals itself in the theologian's epistemological options. The Vatican's declaration seems to stress adherence to the tradition of the Church, while Asian Christians and theologians seem to stress the value of their contextual experience of Asia's religious pluralism. The dilemma posed can also be seen as a struggle between being authentically Christian while at the same time being authentically Asian. This is the double loyalty Christians in Asia have to strive towards. They have to be at once true and obedient to the faith as passed down to them through the missionaries and true and obedient to God speaking to them in and through Asian cultures and religious traditions.

TOWARDS AN INCULTURATED ASIAN CHRISTIANITY

It is in this context that inculturation seems to be the appropriate way ahead. The inculturation of Christianity and the contextualization of the faith seem to be the fundamental task of the Asian Church. The challenge for Asian Christians, therefore, is to develop an inculturated and contextual theology that enables them to relate positively with the religions of

Asia. Such a theology, on the one hand, ought to be able to speak to the issues raised by the Vatican *Declaration* and, on the other, should be able to serve as a blueprint for the Church in Asia to express itself as a truly local Church. In this regard, a contextual theology that is at once faithful to the Christian tradition as well as sensitive to the Asian experience would best serve the Church in Asia. Such a theology has to be facilitative of dialogue since the presence of the other religions of Asia is something that Christians encounter on a massive scale all over Asia. It must, therefore, be a theology of dialogue.

Before attempting to postulate this theology, a framework or theological paradigm or methodology has to be adopted. This will be the task of the next chapters, where we will explore a suitable theological methodology for the purpose of postulating a theology of dialogue. Specifically, the theological method of Edward Schillebeeckx will be looked at since he represents one of the "founding fathers" of the post-Vatican II Church which gave birth to contextual theologies. In order to better appreciate his theology it is important that the context within which he theologized be looked at first. The next chapter, therefore, is dedicated to exploring Schillebeeckx's context and theology in view of adopting principles from his theological method to assist the Asian Church in negotiating the phenomenon of religious pluralism.

3

Schillebeeckx's Theology: Context and Influence

As will be evident later, Schillebeeckx is emphatic that all theology is necessarily situated and contingent upon the context and circumstance in which it arises. In order to appreciate his theology, therefore, it is necessary that we begin by appreciating the context of Schillebeeckx's own life, especially the significant theological and philosophical influences which shaped his thinking. This in turn has also to be done in the context of what was happening in his ecclesial surroundings, especially in connection with the developments of Dutch Catholicism and the Dutch Church, as well as the renewal in the universal Church during the period leading up to the Second Vatican Council.

It will be noted that just as the universal Church was undergoing a transformation in the 1960s, which provided the impetus for the eventual renewal of the Dutch Church, Schillebeeckx himself was also undergoing a conversion with regard to his own approach to doing theology during that same period. As such, we recognize that his life can more or less be divided into two distinct phases. The mid-1960s divides these two phases, during which time he underwent significant transformation in his thinking and method of doing theology.

CONTEXT OF SCHILLEBEECKX'S FORMATION

Much has already been written about Schillebeeckx's life and the context of his experiences. Here we will not go into any length to repeat what is readily available elsewhere, except for aspects that will help in understanding his theology and theological method.

Born in Antwerp in 1914 to a religiously devout Catholic family, Edward Cornelis Florentius Alfonsus Schillebeeckx then grew up in Kortenberg, a city in the predominantly Catholic Flemish territories of Belgium. He was initiated into a very Catholic lifestyle from an early age, attending early morning Mass as well as serving as altar boy from the age of six. Upon completing his primary education he was sent to a Jesuit boarding school in Turnhout, a city within the province of Antwerp. At the age of twenty Schillebeeckx joined the Dominican order in Gent and then moved on to Louvain, where he came under the mentorship of Flemish philosopher Dominic De Petter.

Upon completion of his *philosophicum* in 1938, Schillebeeckx began military service, a period that turned out to be more academic than military since he served as chaplain. Aside from the privilege of free time during which he continued his studies in philosophy, psychology, and sociology, he also met with pastors from other Christian churches and Jewish rabbis. These experiences of the social sciences and the interaction with other religious believers expanded his worldviews and horizons. After this brief stint with the army Schillebeeckx moved back to Louvain in 1939 to begin his *theologicum*. He was ordained a priest in 1941 but continued to live and study in Louvain. He also taught theology at the Dominican house of studies for two years until the end of the Second World War.

After the War, in 1945, Schillebeeckx was sent to Paris, where he spent two years for postgraduate studies. While he was officially at the famous Dominican theological school Le Saulchoir, he also attended lectures at the Universite de la Sorbonne, the Ecole des Hautes Etudes (School of Higher Studies), and the College de France. It was in Paris that he studied with scholars such as the philosophers René Le Senne, Jean Wahl, Louis Lavelle, and Etienne Gilson, as well as Old Testament scholar Eduard Dhorme and patristic scholar Charles Puech. He was also able to make acquaintance with the esteemed ecumenist Yves Congar, as well as with the phenomenologist Maurice Merleau-Ponty and the existentialist Albert Camus. But the scholar who made the most significant impact on Schillebeeckx's life was his fellow Dominican friar Marie-Dominique Chenu.

In 1947 Schillebeeckx returned to Louvain and was appointed professor of theology in the *Studium generale*, where he taught young Dominican friars. He was responsible for all the dogmatic courses, "lecturing on everything from creation to eschatology, a course which he covered two and a half times"[1] during a ten-year period. He was at the same time the Master of Students (the post De Petter had held), which meant being responsible for the spiritual development of the priestly candidates. He was also working on the dissertation he had begun while in France, which he was to complete in 1951 under the supervision of Chenu. Pastorally, he worked as chaplain in the local prison. Later, in 1956, Schillebeeckx was appointed professor in Louvain's Higher Institute for Religious Studies.

The year 1957 marked the beginning of a new phase in Schillebeeckx's life. He was appointed Professor of Dogmatics and the History of Theology in the University of Nijmegen, the Netherlands, a post he took up in January 1958 and he held until his retirement in 1982. In this new assignment he was no longer teaching in a Dominican student house but in a university. His students included mostly mature priests and later even some lay people, including women. He also had more time on his hands since he was no longer spiritual director to a group of young friars. Thus, Schillebeeckx was able to get involved with groups outside the academy and accepted invitations to speak to a variety of groups in different parts of the Netherlands as well as to the media. When the Second Vatican Council was announced Schillebeeckx found himself playing an even greater role, first, in its preparations, and then serving as the principal theologian-consultant to the Dutch bishops.

It was within this context of exposure to the wider society (in the Netherlands) as well as to the wider Church (during and after the Second Vatican Council) that Schillebeeckx turned from being a mere professor of theology in a university into what John Bowden calls "an international theologian's theologian."

CONTEXT OF THE DUTCH CHURCH

Because Schillebeeckx's transition to fame was not without relation to the transitions happening in the Netherlands, an exploration of the Dutch context might reveal interesting correlations. Firstly, it was within this Dutch context that saw the transition of Schillebeeckx's theological approach into one that was both new and refreshing. Secondly, it was also around this same period of the 1960s that the Dutch Church itself under-

---

1. Bowden, *Edward Schillebeeckx*, 31.

went a metamorphosis, an experience that was conceivably different from other European Churches. Most importantly, Schillebeeckx's role in the transition of the Dutch Church is by no means insignificant.

To begin, this metamorphosis can be looked at from different vantage points. For the observer who sees this as a change for the better, the Dutch Church represented "the center for new theological, pastoral, liturgical, catechetical, and structural changes taking place within world Catholicism."[2] For another who perceives this as a period of "disintegration" or "general social collapse," the following would be highlighted: deeply rooted religious practices were either abused or abandoned; quick and sudden end to private confession; Christian marriage practices came under intense criticism; obligatory celibacy for the priesthood was openly questioned; exodus of priests and religious from their ministries (by a relative percentage, which was twice that of the USA and three times that of the world average); decline in the number of ordinations (to as low as only 5 percent of the previous era, as compared to other parts of Europe where it declined to only about 40–50 percent); drop in Sunday church attendance; increase in mixed marriages; increase in divorce rates amongst Catholics; increase in crime rates amongst Catholics (an increase relatively higher than Dutch of other Christian confessions). Either way, the one thing sure is that the changes were radical, even by the standards of post-Enlightenment Europe.

Seen in the context that even as late as the mid-1950s Dutch Catholicism was the most traditional on the European continent, the radical transition becomes even more remarkable. For instance, it is interesting to note that the pre-1960s Dutch Church "had the highest rates for weekly Mass attendance; the lowest rates of defection into the ranks of the unchurched; the strongest opposition to ecumenism with Protestants or socialists; the most faithful adherence to traditionalist birth-control norms; and it was the heaviest per capita exporter of priests, nuns, and religious workers."[3] It is as if all of a sudden something happened that turned the traditional, conservative, insular-looking Dutch Church into one of the most liberal as well as controversial Churches in the world. In the context of the Vatican II renewal the Dutch Church was regarded as "the avant-garde in the international church."

2. Coleman, *Evolution of Dutch Catholicism*, 1.
3. Ibid., 2.

How does one explain this transformation? What were some of the circumstances that facilitated the changes in such a fashion? While it cannot be doubted that the Second Vatican Council played a significant role in the transformation, it was Dutch sociopolitical history that contributed more to the uniqueness and radicality of the changes. First of all, it has to be pointed out that historically, unlike Belgium, which was predominantly Catholic, the Netherlands had for over four centuries been predominantly Calvinist. The Dutch Catholic minority had for the most part of this period defined themselves in contradistinction to Protestantism. Living as a minority community, Dutch Catholics "were subjected to distinct religious and economic disadvantages."[4] This in turn resulted in the community developing stronger bonds amongst themselves as well as developing strategic institutions to look after their own community's welfare. With time the Catholic community grew in numbers as well as in strength, paving the way for an eventual liberation and emancipation.

Furthermore, in the second half of the nineteenth century, arising from the struggle for equal rights, Dutch society was segmented by the practice of what came to be known as *verzuiling* ("pillarization" or "columnization"). This was a system "by which the various ideological groupings (secular or religious) in the Dutch population constructed a complex of associations and institutions in nearly every sector of the society."[5] The main pillars across religious or ideological lines were developed, viz., the Catholics, the Orthodox Calvinists, the Dutch Reformed, the socialists, and the humanist liberals. Each pillar had its own political party, schools, banks, clubs, libraries, hospitals, broadcasting stations, research institutes, trade unions, societies for lawyers and doctors, etc. The identity of each pillar was distinctly maintained and even participation in the public realm was through the pillars. The different religious and ideological groups coexisted very peacefully, if only because there was little reason for interactions. The state-sanctioned policies of segregation isolated one community from another, resulting in insular and ghetto-like developments within each community. This accounts for the rigidity to one's self-identity, which, in the Catholic column, was made manifest in the strict adherence to the Church's teachings. This includes, for ex-

---

4. Ibid., 28.
5. Thurlings, "Pluralism and Assimilation," 82.

ample, the non-practice of mixed marriages and a general suspicion of the non-Catholic world, including all its liberal agendas.

Things took a turn in the 1960s when cracks began to appear in the system. A variety of factors contributed to what is known as the *doorbraak* ("breakthrough"). The German occupation of the country during the Second World War had brought the different columns together in view of fighting a common enemy. The opportunities for discussions and collaboration across the columns led to the elites questioning the continued relevance of the segregation. Moreover, by this time the minority groups had already developed quite successfully and generally felt secure. With this new sense of self-security, particularly within the Catholic group, continued isolation was deemed unnecessary especially since there was already a perception that a certain balance of power had become a reality. Slowly but surely the process of *ontzuiling* ("depillarization") began. The Catholic pillar played a central role since it was the largest single bloc as well as the best organized. Another reason was because Catholicism was itself experiencing internal changes, especially in view of the renewal inaugurated by the Second Vatican Council.

It is therefore not surprising that at the time of Vatican II the Dutch Church was already well poised to undergo its own renewal. The phenomenon of pillarization certainly contributed significantly to this. Specifically, the decades of pillarization had necessitated the training of numerous lay Catholics to help maintain the various Church-based structures within the Catholic column. It also facilitated the development of massive intrachurch communication networks. More importantly, it helped the Catholics of the various parishes and dioceses to think and act in terms of one national Church rather than as disconnected Catholic communities. By the time of the Council there was already in existence numerous national-level institutions such as the Catholic broadcasting station, Catholic newspapers, and Catholic research centers, all of which were at the bidding of the Church's hierarchy, who were also operating as a single entity. Some of these institutions, incidentally, were operating with generous financial subsidies from the state. Thus, during the period leading up to the Second Vatican Council, it was without difficulty that the bishops were able to mobilize the various resources to prepare the people for renewal and, subsequently, to implement the demands of the Council. The efficiency and pace with which these took place even inspired the labeling of the Dutch Church "as a symbolic alternative to Rome" and a "rallying symbol for progressive or traditionalist groups of Catholics."[6]

CONTEXT OF THE RENEWAL OF VATICAN II

Thus, when Schillebeeckx arrived at Nijmegen in 1958 he was entering a Dutch Church that was already fermenting and ready to exercise what Emile Durkheim would call the "collective effervescence." His contributions to the scene were by no means insignificant. Even the conservative *Katholiek Nieuwsblad* acknowledged Schillebeeckx's role in this period of transformation. The group points to what they regard as his "negative influence" on the Church, serving as a public figure in the media as well as providing theological legitimation to some of the practices of the critical or base communities that arose after Vatican II.

More significantly, the Dutch bishops also enlisted the assistance of Schillebeeckx when they were preparing for the Second Vatican Council. In particular, the bishops issued a Christmas letter in 1960, which was made accessible to the world's bishops who were going to participate at the Council. The Dutch bishops ended the letter by acknowledging Schillebeeckx's role in the drafting, which, observers suggest, had the flavor of the "new theology" prevalent in that era. As a result, "the officials of the Holy Office rightly saw me as the real author of the letter," Schillebeeckx said much later. "I had written it from a to z. The letter caused pandemonium, outside the Netherlands as well, and was translated into many languages."[7] On top of that, Schillebeeckx also authored a "commentary" on the Council's preparatory schemas and highlighted the outdated theology that was being employed. Both the Christmas letter and his commentary "had a perceptible influence on the course of the first and decisive term of the Council."[8]

While Schillebeeckx did accompany his bishops to Rome during the period of the Council, he was never appointed an official *peritus* as Cardinal Ottaviani of the Holy Office was opposed to his nomination. In retrospect, this could have been a blessing as it freed Schillebeeckx to be able to deliver lectures to numerous bishops. "Before the decisive vote on the 'two sources schema' at the end of November 1962, which

---

6. Coleman, *Evolution of Dutch Catholicism*, 1.
7. Schillebeeckx, *Happy Theologian*, 17.
8. Schoof, "E. Schillebeeckx," 323.

Schillebeeckx's Theology: Context and Influence 53

in Schillebeeckx's opinion, determined the fate of modern theology, he had already given twenty-three such lectures, thus reaching about 1500 bishops."[9] These lectures were organized by the Dutch Documentation Center (DOC), which was to later become the International Documentary Center (IDOC) for the Council.

The DOC testifies to the command the Dutch Church enjoyed at the Council, as it was the only national episcopacy that was able to provide such an autonomous information center in Rome. The DOC became a sort of meeting ground for progressive theologians as it organized lectures delivered by scholars such as Hans Kung, Karl Rahner, M. D. Chenu, and John Courtney Murray. Thus, Vatican II also afforded Schillebeeckx—as well as others—the opportunity to meet with theologians from all over, including those from other Christian Churches as well as bishops from all over, including those from the mission territories and developing nations. These contacts were not only mutually reinforcing but led to cooperative ventures such as the birth of the reputed post-conciliar theological journal *Concilium*.

CONTEXT OF THE CENTER-PERIPHERY DYNAMICS

In view of the significant role that Schillebeeckx and the Dutch Church played at the Council, it comes as no surprise that when the Council concluded controversies began to arise in the relationship between the Dutch Church, including Schillebeeckx, and the Roman Curial officials. One of the first such conflicts was over the *New Catechism*, a catechism developed from the perspective of the new understandings of theology of the era. The Dutch bishops announced its publication in 1966, citing that the word "new" was not so much in reference to its message but rather to its approach. They note that the message remains constant even as the approach taken is new, reflecting the renewal of the Second Vatican Council. It was the product of several years of collaboration between theologians and "catechists trained in modern pedagogical technique" as well as "ordinary Catholics who had tested the book's materials in discussion-group sessions."[10] Because this new approach seemed excessively liberal to some, the *New Catechism* was contested by conservative groups. Within months it came under investigation by Curial officials. In an attempt to resolve

---

9. Schoof, *Breakthrough*, 239.
10. Coleman, *Evolution of Dutch Catholicism*, 248.

the matter a dialogue session was held between theologians appointed by Rome and those by Dutch bishops. Schillebeeckx was among the latter.

After two years of deliberations Rome acknowledged that the *New Catechism* contained no heresies but only "vague and sometimes infelicitous expressions." Nevertheless, they insisted that it be revised and include "a separate brochure in technical, scholastic language which set out the traditional doctrinal formulations on disputed points." Under Roman pressure the Dutch bishops yielded, though it was by no means a guarantee that independent publishers would abide by the decision. What was more significant was that "it seemed to Dutch theologians that the Roman methods had aimed at undermining the authority of the Dutch bishops by sowing doubts about the orthodoxy of the book they had commissioned."[11]

A second conflict surrounded the convening of the Dutch Pastoral Council. Even before Vatican II ended the Dutch bishops were already talking about having their own national-level council. Hence, in November 1966, the Dutch Pastoral Council officially opened in Nordwijkerhout. Between its opening until the last session in 1970, a total of six plenary sessions were held. The Dutch Pastoral Council was as much a social movement as a Church parliament. Its plenary sessions consisted of all the bishops and elected representatives from the ranks of the clergy, religious, and laity. The laity, consisting of many scholars and specialists, made up the majority of the Council. At the plenary sessions the representatives engaged in "open discussions and voting on issues of pastoral policy such as preaching, ecumenism, peace and justice, the exercise of authority in the church, catechetics, the seminary formation of priests, birth-control, and celibacy."[12] The Pastoral Council was thus an exercise of collegiality and consultation.

In 1970, after a period of experimentation, the Council moved towards making these as more permanent structures within the Church. It came as no surprise that this was met with intense objections from Vatican officials. Rome saw the Dutch model as excessively liberal and not protective enough of the "authority of the bishops and their proper place in the church."[13] Following several rounds of discussion and deliberations

11. Ibid., 250.
12. Ibid., 160–61.
13. Ibid., 180.

between the Dutch bishops and Curial bishops, the former yielded. Their sense of resignation also had to do with the fact that around the same period conservative priests had been appointed as bishops, thus causing a split within the episcopacy.

The first two such appointees, Msgr. Simonis (December 1970) and Msgr. Gijsen (January 1972), were known to have openly opposed the Dutch Pastoral Council while they were priests. It is as if they were appointed by Rome "to combat all new ideas and break up the internal unity of the conference of bishops." With the retirement of more avant-garde bishops and further appointment of conservative bishops, many members of the laity, especially the intellectuals, lost all hope for progress and development and so decided to leave the Church.[14]

Schillebeeckx's role in all of this was not insignificant since he was the personal consultant to Cardinal Alfrink, the prelate of the Dutch Episcopal conference at that time. William Portier even suggests that Schillebeeckx was a "key architect of the experiment of Dutch Catholicism during the period of decolumnization and the council."[15] Thus, when Schillebeeckx himself was personally involved in a conflict with Rome, the perception arose that since he had been so much "involved in all the progressive developments of the Dutch Church, an attack on him was also an attack on them [Dutch bishops]."[16] That accounts for why Schillebeeckx is often "for many the personification of 'Dutch theology.'"[17]

The first process that the Roman Curia initiated against Schillebeeckx, in 1968, was on his views of the Eucharist. It did not go beyond the initial stages and so, officially, Schillebeeckx was not even informed about it. He learned about it from Karl Rahner, as it was Rahner who was designated *relator pro auctore* (advocate) for Schillebeeckx. It was Rahner's task to defend Schillebeeckx, a task he performed admirably with help from his student and assistant Karl Lehmann (who later became a cardinal). When the Dutch bishops officially learned about the investigations through the international media, they issued a statement indicating their support and trust in Schillebeeckx. The case was quashed with a blessing coming from

---

14. Schillebeeckx, *Happy Theologian*, 29.
15. Portier, "Interpretation and Method," 27.
16. Hebblethwaite, *New Inquisition*, 28.
17. Schoof, "Masters in Israel," 943.

no less than Pope Paul VI himself, which he showed by innocuously quoting from a passage of one of Schillebeeckx's writings.

The second time round was not as fortunate for Schillebeeckx. A process was initiated in 1976 following his book *Jesus,* which was then taken all the way to the final stages. Aside from questionnaires to which he had to respond, Schillebeeckx had to eventually go for a "colloquium" in Rome where he faced three theologians appointed by the Congregation for the Doctrine of the Faith. After a two-and-a-half day process they could not find anything by which he could be condemned. At most, some questions remained ambiguous, but nothing was found that was not in accord with the faith, only some elements deemed not in accord with the doctrine of the Church. In any case, the second process evoked a series of protests from scholars and theologians from both the Catholic world as well as the world of other Christian confessions. As Vatican correspondent Peter Hebblethwaite put it, "The Schillebeeckx 'case' turned into the Schillebeeckx 'affair.' The man became a symbol."[18]

The third process initiated against Schillebeeckx, in the year 1984, was on his book *Ministry*. Again, it went through the entire process, which ended with him having to attend another "colloquium," this time not with a team but only with Cardinal Ratzinger, the newly appointed prefect of the CDF. Even though, according to Schillebeeckx, the colloquium was cordial, quite informal, and ended without any condemnation, a note was later published "in which it said that for the Congregation there were still some points of disagreement with the official doctrine of the church, not with the faith."[19]

Schillebeeckx's experiences and conflicts with Rome were by no means political or personal. They were ideological disputes over his theology and theological approaches. His background and influences had much to do with this as they accounted for why his approach to theology differed significantly from that taken by Curial officials of the CDF. A look at some of these influences at this juncture would be in order.

THEOLOGICAL AND PHILOSOPHICAL INFLUENCES

As pointed out earlier, Schillebeeckx's formation went through various phases. One can divide these into two main phases, viz., what shall be

18. Hebblethwaite, *New Inquisition?*, 16.
19. Schillebeeckx, *Happy Theologian*, 39.

called the "early Schillebeeckx" and the "later Schillebeeckx." The dividing line often used is the period around the end of the Second Vatican Council, when "his theology underwent a marked change . . . [especially in the] significant shifts in approach and use of interpretive frameworks."[20]

The theology of his early phase was a result of the influence he received while at Louvain and then later at Paris. The theology of his later phase arose out of his experiences in the Dutch Church, the Second Vatican Council, and especially his exposure to the wider world, including a lecture tour to North America in 1966. These latter experiences led him to undertake an "intensive study of different systems of interpretations: the 'new hermeneutics' of the neo-Heideggerians, Anglo-American analytic philosophy, and the critical theory of the Frankfurt school of social criticism."[21]

The Early Schillebeeckx

This first part of Schillebeeckx's formative influence can roughly be regarded to have begun in the years leading up to the Second World War and ending in the years leading up to the Second Vatican Council. Both events were to shape not only Schillebeeckx's own direction in life but his theological thought as well. His exposure to a number of specific intellectual thought at the time helped provide the necessary tools and methods to process the two events above.

Thomism—Living as he did in an era when Roman Catholicism countered modernity by imposing neo-scholastic thought in all Catholic institutes of higher learning, Schillebeeckx was schooled in the tradition of Thomas Aquinas. Moreover, as a Dominican, he naturally had more exposure to Thomistic thought than to any other theologian. The Thomist revival, which was a development within neo-scholasticism, began around 1860, was enforced by Pope Leo XIII's 1879 encyclical *Aeterni Patris*, and lasted up until the period of Vatican II. Drawing on Aristotelian philosophy, Thomism is basically a philosophical theology that begins on the premise that created beings are in participation with nature as with grace. Because the created human participates in the creator God, it is therefore possible for the human being to know God. As human knowledge is ori-

---

20. Schreiter, *Schillebeeckx Reader*, 5.
21. Ibid.

ented towards being and since the first being is God, human knowledge is oriented finally toward God. This knowledge can only come through creation, which means it can only come through our senses, through the physical realm. Sense experience, therefore, is the primary starting point of all knowledge. Robert Schreiter summarizes it thus: "God communicates with us through the medium of the created world and not through some other channel. That relative optimism means that, sinful and broken though the world may be, it remains the medium for this divine-human communication."[22]

Phenomenology—In the Dominican House of Studies in Louvain, under the mentorship of De Petter, Schillebeeckx was able to study Thomistic philosophy interpreted from the phenomenological tradition. De Petter introduced his students to the thoughts of phenomenologists such as Edmund Husserl, Maurice Merleau-Ponty, and Martin Heidegger. Phenomenology's concern was with analyzing and describing the essential structures of experience and thus focuses on the subject, on the experiential ground of knowledge, and on the analysis of the structures of the "life-world."[23] In order to analyze and to describe, subject-object dualism has to be minimized, if not eliminated altogether. Thus, by the method of phenomenological reduction one attempts to return to the original experience, to consciousness, where there is subject-object unity. Within this tradition Merleau-Ponty's work was the most significant influence on Schillebeeckx and represents the philosophical roots of his use of the term "bodiliness," as well as his emphasis on the concrete and the incarnational in most of his theology. Schillebeeckx's study of this phenomenological tradition then evolved into an interest in the works of existentialist phenomenology, with its emphasis on experience as well as metaphor and narrative, all of which can be discerned from Schillebeeckx's own writings, especially the later ones. De Petter also introduced Schillebeeckx to the work of Karl Adam, which dealt on many theological issues but without the use of scholastic terminology. Adam's theological method extended back beyond the medieval thinkers to the Church Fathers while at the same time incorporating a great deal of modern biblical research. Aside from that, De Petter also encouraged Schillebeeckx to read Hegel, Kant, and Freud, as well as books that had been placed on the *Index Librorum*

22. Ibid., 20.
23. Zaner and Ihde, *Phenomenology and Existentialism*, 21.

Prohibitorum (*List of Prohibited Books*) and so should have been almost inaccessible to students in Catholic theological institutions.

Nouvelle Théologie—The two years Schillebeeckx spent in Paris was yet another opportunity to further his Thomistic studies but this time interpreted from the perspective of the French *Nouvelle Théologie*. Within the Dominicans, Chenu and Congar were the key figures associated with this movement and the concomitant *ressourcement* or "back to the sources" method. This essentially meant reading Thomistic texts with attention paid to the historical setting in which they were produced, i.e., returning to the patristic and medieval sources. This is the historical-critical approach to doing theology, an approach that imprinted on Schillebeeckx that texts and teachings are culturally and historically conditioned. He would later employ this approach in his research on the *Jesus* book except that he returned all the way back to Scripture as the original source. Aside from this, Schillebeeckx was also influenced especially by Chenu's personality and the latter's commitment to works of justice as expressed by Chenu's involvement in the worker-priest movement. It was also through Chenu's work that Schillebeeckx took a greater interest in theology than philosophy. Specifically, "Chenu's fusion of theological research with social-political engagement" interested Schillebeeckx, resulting in him becoming "more and more preoccupied with the relationship between world and church" rather than just be concerned about Church issues.[24]

Thus, if De Petter was to be Schillebeeckx's great master in philosophy, Chenu was acknowledged by him as the greatest theological influence in his life. It is interesting to note that all three of Schillebeeckx's great masters encountered some sort of conflict with the Church's Magisterium—either a local bishop or Rome—at one time or another: Thomas Aquinas in 1277, Dominic De Petter in 1941, and Marie-Dominique Chenu in 1942. Could these also have represented a kind of formative experience for Schillebeeckx as preparation for his own fate?

The Later Schillebeeckx

As alluded to earlier, the mid-1960s represented a turning point for Schillebeeckx in that his writings began to show a marked change in content as well as approach. This is no doubt a result of a variety of factors

---

24. Kennedy, *Deus Humanissimus*, 53.

within his contextual experience during what Ted Schoof terms as "the turbulent decade."[25] Schoof even suggests that Vatican II had an influence upon Schillebeeckx's work in a way experienced by no other theologian. His teaching at Nijmegen was evidence of this in that he began to discuss issues raised by the Council as well as to employ new approaches such as hermeneutics.

Aside from the Council and the turmoil in the Dutch Church at that time, parallel developments in the world such as the increasing secularization of society and the concomitant "theology of secularization" also captured Schillebeeckx's attention. Of significance is John Robinson's little book *Honest to God*. During a lecture tour Schillebeeckx made to North America in 1966 he was also brought face to face with the "death of God" theology. All of these were to affect his subsequent thinking and way of doing theology.

Meantime, Europe, with its student rebellions and other political turmoil, also saw the development of new theological approaches to address the new social realities. Specifically, interest in Marx's work had arisen, which also led to interest in the social sciences, hermeneutics, and other social and critical theories. It is not by accident that during this period, specifically between 1963 and 1974, Schillebeeckx did not write any new book. Those years could be regarded as yet another period of his own formation. We will now review some of the major intellectual influences in this period of his formation.

Hermeneutics—The first of such influences is what has come to be known as the "new hermeneutics." This hermeneutic philosophy represented a significant influence in Schillebeeckx's thought as it offered him an alternative interpretative theory to Thomism. Influenced by Martin Heidegger, it was but "another variant on existentialist phenomenology," which asserted the linguisticality of being as well as "stressed the historical character, or historicity, of being itself."[26] Specifically, truth is conceived of as always in process and pluralistically articulated and so has to be apprehended within the flux of history, of which it itself is also a part. It is not possible, therefore, for an interpreter to fully enter into another historical world as the interpreter is always approaching a text with some pre-understandings. With these pre-understandings the interpreter ques-

---

25. Schoof, "E. Schillebeeckx," 323.
26. Schreiter, *Schillebeeckx Reader*, 21, 99.

tions the text while the text in turn also raises questions to the interpreter. The consequence of this process is the hermeneutical circle. The new hermeneutics was actually post-Heideggerian and saw its elaboration by scholars such as Hans-Georg Gadamer, Paul Ricoeur, Rudolf Bultmann, Gerhard Ebeling, and Ernst Fuchs. The writings of some of these scholars helped shape Schillebeeckx's thinking. His conclusion from studying the new hermeneutics is that "the best way to keep faith alive is not a literal repetition of past texts but their reinterpretation in light of contemporary modes of thought."[27]

Philosophy of Language—The new hermeneutics' stress on the importance of language led Schillebeeckx to study the philosophy of language, including those of the Anglo-American types. The works of the Austrian Ludwig Wittgenstein, who discussed the concept of "language games," as well as the work of the Brit Ian Ramsey, who elaborated on the concept of "disclosure," were useful in providing Schillebeeckx with new vocabulary for his future theological writings. Also called "ordinary language philosophy," its distinguishing mark "is the assertion that meaning is not prior to language as if words merely give form to a pre-existing intention or meaning. Rather, according to this view [of ordinary language philosophy], meaning only becomes apparent at all in virtue of a pre-established and functioning language."[28]

Critical Theory—The next major philosophical influence in Schillebeeckx's life came about as a response to a challenge by a group of young theologians who were students of Johann Baptist Metz. They questioned Schillebeeckx's unquestioning reliance upon the theology of secularization and its over-identification with modern Western culture. They drew on critical theory to protest modern secularism and called for a reassessment of the relationship between theory and practice. As a result, Schillebeeckx delved more fully into the works of the critical theorists. Usually associated with the Marxist-inspired Frankfurt school of social criticism, critical theory set out to explain "the failures of the social revolutions over and against classical Marxism."[29] It is really a form of Western Marxism but focuses more on culture and ideology rather than on the

27. Kennedy, *Schillebeeckx*, 48.
28. Ibid.
29. Ibid., 49.

politics of class struggle and economic history. Critical theory employs the intellectual disciplines of not only economics and politics but also culture and aesthetics in its critique of society and those who dominate it. It is a liberation theory, resolved on liberating the oppressed and the socially and economically subjugated. The early exponents of critical theory were Max Horkheimer and Theodor Adorno. But it was the second-generation theorist Jurgen Habermas whose works Schillebeeckx studied most. As a result of his interactions with critical theory, Schillebeeckx's theology became "more politically responsible, eschatologically orientated, and resolutely attentive to suffering."[30] Concepts that were to appear unsparingly in his later writings, such as "ideology," "ideological critique," "praxis," "orthopraxis," "negative contrast experience," "negative dialectics," etc. are all rooted in critical theory.[31]

Modern Biblical Research—A final but no less important field of influence on Schillebeeckx is modern biblical research, often described in terms of the "quest for the historical Jesus." Stimulated in part by the anti-dogmatic attitude of the post-Reformation era, Protestant scholars were the first to develop modern biblical theology, which espoused the rationalist historical-critical thought of the Enlightenment. The beginning of the "quest" is often traced to eighteenth-century Protestant scholar Herman Reimarus, a German philologist. His works focused on removing the external trappings of the supernatural dogmas surrounding Jesus to differentiate between the "Jesus of history" and the "Christ of faith." Numerous others, all Protestants, continued this strand of research, including scholars such as David Strauss, Adolf von Harnack, and Johannes Weiss. But it was Albert Schweitzer who closed this liberal quest with the publication, at the turn into the twentieth century, of his book *The Quest of the Historical Jesus*. The historical Jesus, he believed, could not be recovered by scientific research of the New Testament documents. Subsequently, Rudolf Bultmann even went so far as to say that such research is not only impossible but also illegitimate. The search for the historical Jesus, Bultmann contends, is no more than an attempt at self-salvation through human intellection.

This stalemate was to last until 1953, when former students of Bultmann, such as Ernst Kasemann, launched what they called the "New

30. Ibid., 51–52.
31. Schreiter, *Schillebeeckx Reader*, 24.

Quest for the Historical Jesus." They argued that unless continuity is traced between the historically ascertained data about Jesus and the Christ-figure of the Gospels, Christians would not be able to respond if their beliefs were regarded as mere myths having no relation to Jesus of Nazareth. Thus began the new quest, employing tools such as form and redaction criticisms. It was this new quest that Schillebeeckx delved into, and he has since been regarded as the first Roman Catholic to employ these studies in a really substantive way to advance theological research.

As will be evident in the next chapter, a lot of the theological and philosophical influences upon Schillebeeckx that we have just discussed reveal themselves in his writings, especially the method by which he does theology. It is this theological method that makes his theology not only unique but also revolutionary, as it offers an alternate paradigm for discerning God's Word and God's will on earth. And it is this method that is of interest to the present research in addressing Christianity's encounter with the world's religions. This will be the task of the next chapter.

4

Schillebeeckx's Theology: Approach and Method

As noted earlier, Schillebeeckx was schooled in the neo-scholastic tradition. Obviously his early theological writings began with this traditional and dogmatic approach. But this was to change in the 1960s on account of his own contextual experiences of Dutch Catholicism, of the renewal of Vatican II, and of the secularization of the West. He then turned to hermeneutics and critical theory, but this turn did not mean he gave up the focus that had occupied him in earlier years. Suffice to say that the neo-scholastic method of doing theology provided the foundations for him to understand differences in approach and to better appreciate the later theological methodologies to which he was exposed

METHOD IN THEOLOGY

Each theological method has its own starting point and, in the words of Bernard Lonergan, its own "normative pattern of recurrent and related operations yielding cumulative and progressive results."[1] As we explore Schillebeeckx's earlier theological methodology we do so realizing that it enables us to not only understand the cumulative and progressive results the neo-scholastic method yields but also the Vatican declaration *Dominus Iesus*. In an assessment of the document, Filipino theologian Jose de Mesa's primary comment is that "the over-all theological method that it espouses and follows ... is that of Neo-Scholasticism."[2] The espousal of such a method significantly shapes the theology of *Dominus Iesus* and thus accounts for its incompatibility with Asian theologies, which by

---

1. Lonergan, *Method in Theology*, 4.
2. Mesa, "Historical and Cultural," 221.

and large are developed using a contextual and inculturated theological methodology.

It is the task of this chapter to look at how theological assertions are a function of theological methods, in view of appreciating why Vatican officials have difficulties with theologies of religious pluralism and how Schillebeeckx's theological method can help us understand and appreciate Asian theologies of inculturation. We begin by looking at Schillebeeckx's neo-scholastic method and then move on to look at the hermeneutical-critical method he developed in his later years. To facilitate a better understanding of the neo-scholastic method it is necessary that we begin by exploring briefly its antecedent, namely, the scholastic method.

Anselm of Canterbury's *Proslogion*, which clearly appeals to reason and emphasizes the role of logic in theology, "anticipates the best of scholastic theology."[3] His two mottos of *fides quaerens intellectum* ("faith seeking understanding") and *credo ut intellegam* ("I believe, in order that I may understand") advance the insight that "while faith came before understanding, the content of faith was nevertheless rational." The two dictums "established the priority of faith over reason, just as they asserted the entire reasonableness of faith."[4] With this, Anselm bridged the previous generation's spiritual theology of the monasteries—which emphasized "the sufficiency of faith as expressed in Sacred Scripture"—to the new theology of the schoolmen (or scholastics) of the twelfth century—which emphasized "the need for critical reflection on that faith, using not only Sacred Scripture, but the writings of the early Christian witnesses, theologians, and philosophers, even non-Christian philosophers such as Aristotle."[5]

While there are certainly differences amongst the scholastics (Bonaventure, Duns Scotus, William of Ockham, Thomas Aquinas, etc.), all advocate "the power of reason" in the "understanding of the mysteries of faith" and in the construction of "some overarching synthesis of the whole Christian doctrinal system." An "intellectual optimism," therefore, characterizes the scholastics' method.[6] For Thomas Aquinas (undoubtedly the foremost of the scholastic theologians), "the act of faith is essentially

---

3. McGrath, *Christian Theology*, 43.
4. Ibid., 49.
5. McBrien, *Catholicism*, 45.
6. Ibid., 46.

an act of the intellect, but not just any act of the intellect. It is thinking with assent."[7] While clearly emphasizing the cognitive dimensions of faith, Thomas also posits the centrality of God's action in the assent of faith: "Revelation . . . is that saving act by which God furnishes us with the truths which are necessary for our salvation." Occurring in history, revelation is that divine initiative which facilitates the understanding of revealed truths, the climax of which is the incarnation of God in Jesus Christ. Faith, on the other hand, is the supernatural assent to these divine truths by means of a reasoning process that is "an ascending movement of the mind from creatures to God."[8] The task of theology, or *sacra doctrina*, is to enable the intellect to draw conclusions from the knowledge of God's revelation so that the will can make an assent of faith.[9]

Without denying the importance of Augustine's thesis that spiritual assent and purification are requisite to knowledge of God and of the faith, the scholastics advanced the thesis that "our sense experience of the visible and the concrete" are also ways by which we know God.[10] The experience, however, has to be guided by the authority of Sacred Scripture, which the scholastics view as the ultimate authority of all theological endeavors. For Thomas Aquinas, "the canonical Scriptures have . . . a primal significance and authority" while the use of the doctors of the Church are "only with probable effect" and the reliance on the "philosophers only as extrinsic and probable." Extra-scriptural sources are only employed inasmuch as they assist in ascertaining the revealed truths as contained in Scriptures. The entire procedure is conducted through the process of natural reasoning.[11] The instructional methods employed during the scholastic period were that of *quaestio* ("question")—especially during the high period of scholasticism—and of *disputatio* ("disputation")—especially in late scholasticism. The use of these methods often entailed lively academic debates, encouraged divergent thinking, and resulted in numerous viewpoints and opinions.

The scholastic method dominated Catholic theology for the most part of the medieval period. At the beginning of the nineteenth century it

7. Ibid., 35.
8. Ibid., 240–41.
9. Fiorenza, "Systematic Theology, 21.
10. Ibid., 46.
11. Ibid., 24.

had all but ceased to be significant. The Renaissance and Enlightenment, which saw changes in the understandings of epistemology, metaphysics, and even to the very understandings of the scientific method, "shattered the unity of philosophy and theology in eighteenth-century scholasticism."[12] This in part was responsible for the end of scholastic influence.

THE NEO-SCHOLASTIC METHOD

Around the year 1830, a campaign to restore scholasticism began with Taparelli, rector of the Jesuit Roman college, with the help of his fellow Jesuits, Liberatore and Kleutgen. But it was really Pope Leo XIII, a former student of Taparelli, who brought scholasticism back into mainstream Catholic theology. With his 1879 encyclical *Aeterni Patris*, Leo XIII instructed that Thomism be the only philosophy and theology that is to be taught in all Catholic seminaries.[13] Thus began the influence of neo-scholasticism, or neo-Thomism, to be exact. Among the distinguished neo-scholastics the first half of the twentieth-century produced were Garrigou-Lagrange, Sertillanges, Chenu, Rousselot, Marechal, Gilson, Bouillard, Maritain, and de Lubac. This neo-scholastic influence was to last right until just before the period of the Second Vatican Council, during which time the *Nouvelle Théologie* also came into ascendancy.

Among the neo-scholastics' undertakings was the defense of Catholicism against the two heresies of the time: "the fideism of Protestantism and the rationalism of philosophy."[14] Protestant fideism emphasized the total absoluteness of God and of God's revelation in Jesus Christ. Grace is given freely to human beings despite their inaptness and the sinfulness of the human condition and it is by "faith alone" (*sola fides*) that one is saved. Rationalism (supported also by Protestant thinkers—albeit of the liberal strand—such as Kant, Hegel, and Schleiermacher), on the other hand, stressed the positive implications of the human condition and regarded revelation as no more than the human rational effort to comprehend God and the ultimate mysteries. Reason alone suffices for the attainment of salvation. Fideism and rationalism, therefore, were the dual challenge posed to Catholic theology, the response of which was given through neo-scholastic thought.

12. McCool, *Catholic Theology*, 27–29.
13. McCool, "Neo-Scholasticism," 714.
14. Mesa and Wostyn, *Doing Theology*, 12.

Steering a middle course, the neo-scholastics distinguished between the "fact of revelation" and the "truth of revelation." Against the fideists, the "fact of revelation" countered the thesis that "only faith counts when we speak of our relationship with God." Rather, God's revelation is ongoing and continues even until today; this is a fact. Against the rationalists, the "truth of revelation" countered the thesis that reason alone is sufficient, for the content of God's communication "could only be accepted in faith on the authority of the revealing God." This truth is independent of the reasoning process. In light of these two concerns, neo-scholasticism developed an "intellectualistic notion of revelation and faith," with stress on the revelation of a "body of supernatural truths."[15]

Influenced greatly by the writings of the Parisian theologian Denis Petau, neo-scholastic theologians conceived of theology as a deductive science: "Theology advances in knowledge by deducing conclusions from premises of faith by means of premises of reason. Philosophy is the intermediate link within a syllogistic process of theology."[16] Inasmuch as theology consists of deductive, syllogistic theological conclusions it is a scientific discipline. Such a method constituted the basis for the development of the neo-scholastic handbooks or manuals of theology.

The theological manuals were neo-scholastics' distinctive contribution to theology. These manuals had a uniform approach and methodology, which can be described briefly as: (i) set forth a Catholic teaching, (ii) appeal to Scripture and Tradition, and (iii) explicate on the thesis of the teaching. The starting point of the neo-scholastics' method of theology, therefore, is Church teaching. Neo-scholastic theologians regard Church teaching as the "immediate rule of faith" (*regula fidei proxima*). "It was this teaching that provided a clear rule and definite standard enabling believers to ascertain those truths contained in Scriptures and traditions." The second step in the neo-scholastics' method is that of verifying the Church teaching by recourse to the sources of faith, viz., Scripture and Tradition. This step often sees passages from Scripture and the early Christian writers being lifted out of their contexts to serve as prooftexts for the proposed Church teaching. In effect Scripture and Tradition were considered as no more than the "remote rule of faith." The third step "sought to give a systematic explication of the thesis and thereby lead to a

---

15. Ibid., 12–13.
16. Fiorenza, "Systematic Theology," 29–30.

more profound understanding of its truth." Church teachings (the starting point), affirmed by Scripture and Tradition (the second step), are in this third step "illumined through philosophical reflection." In this step of systematic reflection, examples, analogies, and comparisons are employed, with the aim of explaining the Church doctrine or teaching more fully, especially in view of making it relevant and applicable to contemporary culture.[17]

As can be observed from the foregoing discussion, the neo-scholastics' method is distinct from the traditional scholastic method of the Middle Ages. Significantly, the instructional method changed: from one of *quaestio* and *disputatio* to one of presentation of a thesis. This new method, which begins with theses about Church teachings, significantly shapes the outcome of theology as it provides little space for divergent thinking nor conflicting views. The theses are often presented in very concise and exact formulas, allowing for little variance or differences in interpretation. Another difference is that of the role accorded to Scripture. While medieval scholasticism took Scripture as starting point, the neo-scholastics came to regard Scripture as merely a secondary source to verify Church teaching. This in part was a reaction against the Reformation's appeal to Scripture, which the neo-scholastics argued can often be misinterpreted. Instead, the teaching authority of the Church was given greater prominence. This falls in line with the First Vatican Council's proclamation on papal infallibility, which effectively elevated the status of the teaching authority of the Church.

For the neo-scholastic method to be effective the official Church teaching to be proposed had to be carefully promulgated, delineating distinctively its parameters and where it is binding and/or obligatory. "Theological propositions were classified regarding their centrality to faith, their degree of certitude, and their corresponding censure."[18] The hierarchy of truths takes on primal significance. The preciseness of the propositions and classifications also corresponds to the Cartesian emphases on clarity and exactness. They make clear the parameters within which theological debates and discussions can be entertained. Dissent and disagreement, if allowed, are carefully regulated so as not to steer beyond the set parameters. Philosophy is used, not so much as a chal-

17. Ibid., 31–33.
18. Ibid., 31.

lenge or critique of the Church teaching, but in the service of theological reflection. As a result, the neo-scholastic method, which takes as starting point the official teachings of the Church, has as its end point the same doctrines proposed. Declared in the form of precise and exact formulas of faith, the doctrines are then easily used for preaching and teaching purposes.

SCHILLEBEECKX'S NEO-SCHOLASTIC BEGINNINGS

As was discussed earlier, Schillebeeckx had his formative years under the influence of neo-scholasticism—as did most other Catholic theologians of the pre-Vatican II era. His first major publication, *De Sacramentele Heilseconomie* ("The Sacramental Economy of Salvation")—a revised version of a part of his 1951 doctoral dissertation—was really a reflection on Thomas Aquinas's teachings. It was subtitled "A Theological Reflection on St. Thomas' Teaching on Sacraments in the Light of Tradition and the Current Sacramental Problematic." "Methodologically, the work is dogmatic, which is to say, its primary source and starting point is an examination of ecclesiastical dogmas and teachings."[19] That notwithstanding, Schillebeeckx's theology was a Thomism with a difference.

Firstly, it was a Thomism read from an existentialist phenomenological perspective—as influenced by De Petter and others. Robert Schreiter points out that even after Schillebeeckx abandoned De Petter's framework, "he continued to stress the absolute priority of God's grace over human endeavor, the ultimate inability of any conceptual system to express completely the richness of human experiences, and God's infinite love for creation."[20] Secondly, it was also a Thomism read within the general ambience of the French *Nouvelle Théologie*, as influenced especially by Chenu and Congar.

William Hill suggests that the

> two lasting convictions from this experience were an understanding that God's self-disclosure is not a mere occurrence of the past but a continuing phenomenon mediated through contemporary cultural realities and an awareness that the recovery of the thought of Aquinas meant a reconstruction of the historical context in which it came to birth, which allowed that thought to reemerge in

---

19. Kennedy, *Schillebeeckx*, 61.
20. Schreiter, *Schillebeeckx Reader*, 2.

a way that challenged the rationalistic and conceptualist interpretation being put upon by neo-Thomism.[21]

These schools of thought, which constituted Schillebeeckx's initial formative years, continued to wield an influence on his later writings in that they "retained central features of De Petter's philosophy, historical *ressourcement*, and phenomenology."[22]

With that as background, Schillebeeckx was actually intellectually well poised for a transformation in his theological method when he encountered the contextual realities of the 1960s. That notwithstanding, he still underwent what Philip Kennedy terms a "momentous philosophical turnabout." "He came to the momentous realization that the ultimate meaning of human existence (universality) cannot be accounted for by a particular purely theoretical perspective."[23] How can God, who is absolute, eternal, and universal, and whose salvation is for all persons and for all times, be perceived and apprehended by a human being, a religion, or a theological system that is relative, limited, and particular, and subject to the contingencies of history and culture? In other words, theology must address the issue of the universal vis-á-vis the particular, of explaining "how that which is absolute, true, and the totality of meaning (universal/God) can be perceived in that which is limited and particular (human history)."[24]

Schillebeeckx was to later argue that, at best, the human being can only anticipate what this God or absolute mystery is. The human being obtains a mere semblance of what the absolute stands for and especially how the absolute grants meaning and salvation. This anticipation is effected by means of actual human actions, in the praxis of Christian living, and sustained by the hope that accompanies such actions. Schillebeeckx posits a turn from a "theoretical participation in" to a "practical anticipation of" the absolute meaning of life, of God, and of the world. "This, then, is the most significant switch in Schillebeeckx's philosophical assumptions: a turnabout from asserting that the universality/particularity interrelationship can be explained in terms of a cognitive, theoretical apprehension of

---

21. Hill, "Human Happiness," 9.
22. Kennedy, *Schillebeeckx*, 42–43.
23. Ibid.
24. Ibid., 43.

universality by a particularity, to asserting that whatever is universal can only be practically and partially anticipated in human actions."[25]

This new awareness of the historicity and finitude of the human condition confirmed even more clearly for Schillebeeckx that any apprehension of the absolute mystery of God is at best an approximation. Moreover, any apprehension of this absolute mystery is but one perspective of the absolute. When expressed in language and concepts it is a perspective very much shaped by the history and culture within which those concepts and language developed. In short, the theologian's conclusions are culturally and historically conditioned. Hermeneutics, therefore, is imperative and central to the task of theology.

TOWARDS A CATHOLIC USE OF HERMENEUTICS

The year 1967 is often regarded as the turning point for Schillebeeckx, as far as his method of doing theology is concerned. In an epilogue in the book compiling five essays he presented during his United States lecture tour that year, Schillebeeckx points to two experiences that brought about this turn to hermeneutics. The first was his direct encounter with American pragmatism, in the secularism of the United States, and especially with the "death of God" theologians. The second was his encounter with a group of French university chaplains who espoused a typically anti-pragmatic *spiritualite*. The radically differing "worlds" of the two groups—"the world of 'efficiency' and the world of *spiritualite*," respectively—induced Schillebeeckx to rethink the problem of religion (in particular Christianity) and the problems of the contemporary world (in particular secularization).[26] In fact, he had actually begun his lecture series with these words of reflection:

> It is clear that Christian revelation in its traditional form has ceased to provide any valid answer to the questions about God asked by the majority of people today, nor would it appear to be making any contribution to modern man's real understanding of himself in this world and in human history. It is evident that more and more people are becoming increasingly unhappy and dissatisfied with the traditional Christian answers to their questions. It is their questions about God himself which are involved above all, and there is unmistakable evidence of a growing desire everywhere for

25. Ibid.
26. Schillebeeckx, "Epilogue," 169–70.

new answers to be given to new questions concerning him. The situation requires us to speak of God in a way quite *different* from the way in which we have spoken of him in the past. If we fail to do this, we ourselves shall perhaps still be able to experience God in outmoded forms, but clearly our own witness of and discussion of God will be met with headshaking disbelief as mumbo-jumbo.[27]

It was the reality of this "mumbo-jumbo" that prompted Schillebeeckx to warn that "present-day theology, both conservative and progressive, will render the problem of faith more acute if it does not devote itself first of all to a serious search for a real hermeneutics of history which analyzes the ontological conditions making possible the retention of an authentic identity of faith *within* the reinterpretation of faith, a reinterpretation which in turn is necessary because of man's situation in history."[28] Thus began Schillebeeckx's journey as a theologian in hermeneutical investigation. A more practical reason for this is that in 1966, having just come out of the Second Vatican Council, Schillebeeckx began teaching a course on hermeneutics at Nijmegen.[29]

In the seminal essay entitled "Towards a Catholic Use of Hermeneutics," Schillebeeckx begins by stating categorically that "the new hermeneutics has arisen from the quest for a method of proclaiming the evangelical message which will bring it home to twentieth-century man: a proclamation which will on the one hand remain faithful to the word of God and on the other hand will allow that word to ring out in a way which does not by-pass the reality of his life."[30] In this essay frequent reference is made to the works of existential philosopher-theologians such as Martin Heidegger, Rudolf Bultmann, and Hans-Georg Gadamer, as well as historical theologians such as Wolhart Pannenberg and Jurgen Moltmann. The former are scholars often associated with the "new hermeneutics." Issues of authenticity and continuity with the Christian tradition are important, as are issues of meaning and relevance to contemporary society. While, on the one hand, there is a concern for whether "the Christian faith is emerging intact," on the other, it cannot be denied that these reinterpretations of the Christian message are indeed helping "the faith to

27. Ibid., 53.
28. Ibid., 86.
29. Schoof, "'Masters in Israel," 950.
30. Schillebeeckx, "Towards Catholic Hermeneutics," 3.

pass unscathed through its present-day crisis."[31] This, then, is the challenge of hermeneutics: to be traditionally faithful as well as contemporarily relevant.

THE HERMENEUTICAL PROBLEM

Schillebeeckx introduces the need for hermeneutics by pointing to God's dialogue with the world. This dialogue is more commonly referred to as revelation or the Word of God. The "word from God," Schillebeeckx asserts, does not come to us "without alloy," "coming down to us, as it were, vertically in a purely divine statement." It is always in an interpreted form. Even the Old and New Testaments are already in interpreted forms; interpreted by the biblical redactors who were bearing witness "interpretatively to God's saving actions in Israel and in the man Jesus, the Christ, the foundation of their hope for a renewed world."[32] This witness of the biblical authors was in turn reinterpreted through the centuries of Christian history: from Tertullian and Augustine through Nicea and Chalcedon; from Thomas Aquinas and Trent through the Reformation and Schleiermacher; and, if we take a contemporary stance, from Vatican II and Schillebeeckx right down to the present, including *Dominus Iesus* and Asian theologies.

In essence, God's Word—made available to us through "a conversation between men," which is "human dialogue in which God gave himself to be understood"—is always given within a particular context and history. It is "necessarily *situated*—it had a social setting, a living historical context."[33] Its interpretation is contingent upon the context, employing ideas, concepts, languages, and media that abide by that particular setting and culture. Herein lies the hermeneutical problem: How can "a message of God to men expressed and interpreted in a specific historical situation of the past [become] the norm for, and the test of, *our* Christian faith today—a faith that is experienced in a totally different situation?" The problem arises because, according to Schillebeeckx, the only way hermeneutics is possible is to reinterpret the past through the medium and pre-understandings of the present. There is no way a finite being can transcend time in order to interpret the past as it is. The "norm," e.g.,

31. Ibid., 4.
32. Ibid., 5.
33. Ibid.

Chalcedon, used to interpret a later context is already an interpretation which is as much culturally and historically conditioned as the interpretation which it seeks to give. How then can Chalcedon function as norm? This is precisely the hermeneutical problem, in that "the contemporary scene with its understanding of its own existence is a 'hermeneutical' situation, and it is only within this and from this situation (certainly not outside it or from above) that we can understand in faith what the biblical message itself gives us to understand."[34]

Schillebeeckx posits that at the roots of this hermeneutical problem is the historicity of human existence. The interpreter, attempting to understand the God-human dialogue of history, is never outside of or above this history. S/he is a part of the object of the historical phenomenon that is to be interpreted. "All understanding is therefore a form of self-understanding." The interpreter's whole person, self-existence, and pre-understandings are significant elements in the hermeneutical process. It is within the context of the interpreter's own new "hermeneutical situation" that a question is asked of Scripture and Tradition. Scripture and Tradition, which have evolved out of their own "hermeneutical situations" and cultural settings, are now being used to respond to the questions of the new situation, which are conditioned by the interpreter's present realities and contextual experience. Hence, Scripture and Tradition can only provide an "answer" inasmuch as it is understood within the interpreter's contemporary context, with its concomitant language, culture, and symbol systems. This answer is to a great extent "determined by the question, which is in turn confirmed, extended, or corrected by the answer. A new question then grows out of this understanding." This is what is known as the "hermeneutical circle," which "continues to develop in a never-ending spiral." By "never-ending," it simply means that the process goes on indefinitely. As human beings, we will never ever have the final word—save, perhaps, in the eschaton.[35]

The entire dynamics, commonly held to have originated with Bultmann, is known in Protestant circles as the "hermeneutical problem." It is also evidenced in Catholic theology even though presented as the "development of dogma." After all, even within Catholicism, any new dogmatic formulation implies that "the Biblical view of Christ has

---

34. Ibid., 6–7.
35. Ibid., 7–8.

been reinterpreted in the light of the Church's experience." For example, Chalcedonian Christology implies a rereading of the doctrine of Christ within "the secular and social situation in the fifth century and, what is more, in such a way that this new interpretation really expresses precisely the *same* datum of faith that is promised to us in the Bible and no other."[36] Every new setting is a new "hermeneutical situation," from which and through which we are to reinterpret God's Word. Moreover, the new interpretation represents for us the fullness of the faith, as it was in the beginning, is now, and ever shall be. It is the same dogmatic faith which has been expressed differently over the years, as well as in different cultural contexts. It is in relation to this that Catholicism claims that dogma "develops."

HERMENEUTICAL PRINCIPLES

Convinced by the thesis of human being's historicity, Schillebeeckx cautions that the literal repetition of Scripture and Tradition in order to address present-day issues is tantamount to an act of unfaithfulness to the Word of God. Scripture and Tradition have to be reinterpreted for them to be relevant to present-day realities, as well as faithful to the living message of God's Word. Interrogating this thesis entails addressing the following: How are we to know that a particular interpretation is faithful to the living message? What are the hermeneutical criteria to ensure this faithfulness? "Indeed," Schillebeeckx acknowledges, "the identity of faith, the problem of the relationship between Scripture and present-day preaching by the Church, is at stake."[37]

In addressing the foregoing concerns, Schillebeeckx begins by exploring the historical dimension of human beings' existence as believers. He does this by examining what he calls the "hermeneutics of history" so as to have a better understanding of the notion of faith in the context of history. Concentrating on one aspect of this, namely, that of the "hermeneutical significance of the *distance in time* in what we may call '*historical* interhuman encounter,'" Schillebeeckx discusses three points: (i) the past in the light of the present; (ii) both the present and the past within the sphere of the promise; and (iii) permanence in the present, past, and future.

36. Ibid., 6–7.
37. Ibid., 20.

The Past in the Light of the Present—The distance in time between the past and the present has often been regarded as "an obstacle to objective interpretation of texts and of history that had to be overcome." With Ricoeur, Aron, Marrou, and Gadamer, Schillebeeckx suggests that it is precisely this "distanciation" which constitutes the "ontological condition that makes this interpretation possible." Because this distance in time is not a void but an interim filled by the continuity of tradition, it helps shape the hermeneutical situation of the present, from which we question the text of the past. This evokes the hermeneutical problem. "Ultimately, it *is* the hermeneutical problem."[38]

The interpreter enters the hermeneutical situation with pre-understandings and presuppositions that have arisen as a result of the interaction between Tradition and contemporary experience. Consciously acknowledging these pre-understandings, the interpreter approaches the text in view of forging an understanding of it, as well as correcting any part of the pre-understandings where this applies. The authority of the text is presumed: "The text itself is binding and acts as a norm to understanding." It can only be understood "in its application to the present" and not "in a return to the original period." "If an earlier truth is to be preserved in accordance with its original intention, it must be reformulated in the light of the present and interpreted differently."[39] Each new hermeneutical situation warrants a new and different interpretation of the text. This is done through what Gadamer calls the "fusion of horizons." Schillebeeckx describes it thus: "Hermeneutics requires us to design a *historical* frame of reference which is distinct from our *present* frame of reference and thus to become conscious of the other as different within the fusion of the two spheres (since historicity is one great evolving process)—that is understanding the past."

Both the Present and the Past within the Sphere of the Promise—Aside from the importance of the past and the present in hermeneutics, Schillebeeckx also points to the significance of "future possibilities," that which is "new and completely *unprecedented*." Against Bultmann and the other philosophers of humanities, but with Moltmann and Pannenberg, Schillebeeckx reminds that the "biblical primacy of the future" cannot be passed over in the hermeneutical endeavor. The future, which cannot be

---
38. Ibid., 23–24.
39. Ibid., 26, 30.

interpreted, "has to be realized" and ought to bring "something new into being." "Every dogma must have an orientation towards the future and be open to the sphere of the future." Truth becomes "something whose fullness belongs to the future." It is a future promise, providing a frame of reference for the interpretation of the present and the past.

The Bible testifies to this future of God's promise. Hence, any orthodox interpretation of God's Word must be accompanied by orthopraxis, for "it is only in the sphere of action—of doing in the faith—that orthodox interpretation can be inwardly fulfilled." The Tradition, or "deposit of faith," is as much "the promise already realized in Christ" as is "a promise-for-us, with the result that interpretation becomes 'hermeneutics of praxis.'" The task of hermeneutics cannot end with the interpretation of the past on the basis of the present but must continue into the future, through orthopraxis. The hermeneutical task, therefore, entails the "doing of the faith" in order to realize God's promise, the Word of God, and, in so doing, "*making* dogma true." "Ultimately it is only in and through this historical realization that dogma is interpreted authentically and that the identity of the faith is, thanks to God's promise, guaranteed in continuing history."

Permanence in the Present, Past, and Future—A third aspect of the hermeneutics of history, which, according to Schillebeeckx, the "new hermeneutics" of not only Bultmann but also Gadamer, Pannenberg, and Moltmann is lacking in, has to do with the "consciousness of time." While implying a certain "transcendence of temporality," it does not in any way suggest that we are able to escape time. On the contrary, our historicity implies a real "openness in our temporality," a sense of transhistorical and human transcendence. Within this hermeneutical situation there endures "an aspect of permanence, a dynamic self-identity which cannot in itself be expressed." This self-identity, which is beyond conceptualization, is the "*objective perspective* of faith." It is "brought to light and expressed *in* reinterpretation as it were by a circuitous route (via the interpretative aspect of the act of faith), with the consequence that it becomes a power for action which is directed towards the future." This inexpressible *objective perspective* is "the ever present *mystery* of promise—the mystery which is not uttered, which is everywhere reaching towards expression but in itself is never thought." This *mystery*, "which gives itself in history, [is that which] ensures the identity of the faith *in* the Church's successive interpretations of the faith."

The last statements notwithstanding, Schillebeeckx also points out that "there are no formulae of faith which are, as formulae, enduringly valid, capable of transmitting the living faith to men of all ages." Lest this be construed as "relativism," he quickly adds that "we do not possess the absolute which acts as an inner norm to our faith in an absolute way; we possess it only within our historical situation." This is because, as "pilgrims on the way, we live historically in the absolute, orientated towards the absolute, because this absolute embraces us in grace, without our being able to embrace it."

By way of conclusion, Schillebeeckx advocates that "we should not be afraid of serious attempts to reinterpret the faith." More importantly, one must keep in mind that "the correctness of these interpretations cannot be tested simply by setting earlier formulae of faith against them, since these too always require interpretation and have still to be *made true*." Our task as believers striving to be faithful to the promise of the gospel is to *reinterpret*: "to present the original Dialogue (a living prophecy!) again and again, and above all to put it into action and to let it be heard as the word of God in constantly changing situations in life." Such is the task of hermeneutics and such is the task of theology. Such also is the task of the Church.

HERMENEUTICAL EXTENSION THROUGH CRITICAL THEORY

Schillebeeckx was to later assert that it is only within the framework of a "free dialogue" that truth, which is "inwardly oriented towards universal consent and cannot be bound by restricting qualifications," can be sought. "The whole of hermeneutic science is ultimately based on the possibility of mutual understanding or agreement."[40] In this regard, the Enlightenment, with its accent on the principles of rationality and freedom, brought to conscious awareness the possibility that institutional structures and repressive regimes can tend towards restricting free dialogue. To protect their own vested interests the authoritarian traditions and power holders of such institutional structures obstruct the free dialogue which alone can facilitate the search for truth. Reflecting on this, Schillebeeckx asserts: "The need to break through or to change those structures may therefore be an essential aspect of the hermeneutic process, if it is to lead eventually to general consent or to mutual understanding."[41]

40. Schillebeeckx, *Understanding of Faith*, xi–xiii.
41. Ibid.

Schillebeeckx turned to critical theories in an attempt to explore the "practical and critical interest in structures which will make freedom possible." He paid special attention to critical theory's interest in the relationship between theory and praxis. His primary source of reference was the Frankfurt school of Max Horkheimer and Theodor Adorno, and, outside this school, Ernst Bloch. But it was Jurgen Habermas, the second-generation scholar of the Frankfurt school, whose work most influenced Schillebeeckx.[42] From the outset it has to be mentioned that this turn to Critical Theory is by no means a rejection of philosophical hermeneutics. It is, rather, an extension to include the critical and political dimensions of hermeneutics. Referring to Marx's famous quotation that "philosophers interpret the world, but the point is to change it," Schillebeeckx posits, "To say that the world has to be changed implies a certain interpretation of reality and is itself already an interpretation." In other words, critical theory is another form of hermeneusis, but one that insists on praxis. Its starting point is a "fundamental ethical option in favor of emancipation and freedom." It proceeds within a "hermeneutical circle" that "implies a philosophy of man and this in turn presupposes an implicit interpretation of our humanity."[43]

The classic debate between Gadamer and Habermas contributed significantly to Schillebeeckx's turn to critical theories. Pointing out that Gadamer—"the premier theoretician of the new hermeneutics"—was primarily concerned with "the tradition and its transmittal in his hermeneutics" and so with the "interpretation of the *meaning* found in tradition," Habermas argues that such a process "did not deal with the fact that history is also full of non-meaning: untruth, violence, and repression of competing meanings." While "history is an insane complex of sense and nonsense,"[44] the new hermeneutics perpetuates only one tradition, namely, "the one which legitimated those in power: the tradition of the victors, not the victims." Habermas's critical theory draws upon the insights of the two great masters of suspicion, Marx and Freud. "The new hermeneutics only retrieved the tradition of meaning of the dominant group in society (Marx) for the sake of keeping the present society stable and in continuity with that past meaning (Freud)." With these insights

---

42. Ibid., xii–xiii.
43. Ibid., 124–25.
44. Ibid., 128.

Schillebeeckx advances the importance of ideology critique as "an ideology-critical analysis belongs to the essence of hermeneutical theology, precisely on the basis of fidelity to the Word of God."[45] It has to be pointed out that Schillebeeckx regards "ideology" as "something positive which, however, can come to manifest pathological traits." Positively, it refers to the "images, ideas and symbols which a society creates to give an account of its own identity." This function becomes pathological when it is "distorted, manipulated, and monopolized by dominating groups in society" as a means of "maintaining dominant interests," thus rendering a "false group consciousness."[46]

Critical theory's emancipative concern brought to the fore issues of non-meaning or nonsense. With Adorno and his "principle of non-identity," Schillebeeckx recognized that there was not a necessary correspondence between reason and reality. Human history, replete with non-meaning such as suffering, injustice, and oppression, often defies attempts at explanation and interpretation. There is really no satisfactory explanation that can render life's negativity meaningful. This principle of non-identity undergirds much of Adorno's philosophy and was formulated as *negative dialectics*.[47] While Adorno's was a critical negativity devoid of any affirmative characteristics, Schillebeeckx designated it with "a positive power which continues to exert constant pressure in order to bring about a better world, without humanity itself being sacrificed in the process."[48]

Surmising that "a commitment to the threatened *humanum*" is common to all persons of good will and "constitutes the universal pre-understanding" of all contemporary anthropologies, Schillebeeckx posits that "a sphere of meaning is revealed in the negative experiences of contrast." This occurs when a situation of negativity is accompanied by a positive experience of hope, "expressed in critical opposition to what is inhuman in the situation."[49] This eschatological hope, in light of *negative contrast experiences*, is that which enables critical resistance, evoking the protest, "No! It can't go on like this; we won't stand for it any longer!"

---

45. Ibid., 106, 114.
46. Schreiter, *Schillebeeckx Reader*, 113.
47. Kennedy, *Deus Humanissimus*, 239.
48. Schillebeeckx, "Epilogue," 191.
49. Schillebeeckx, *Understanding of Faith*, 65.

Schillebeeckx explains, "A negative experience would not be a contrast experience, nor could it excite protest, if it did not somehow contain an element of positive hope in the real possibility of a better future."[50]

Challenged by critical theory's hope-filled promise, Schillebeeckx concludes that "hermeneutical theology must be inspired by a practical and critical intention." This in turn implies that orthopraxis is "an essential element of the hermeneutical process." It is thus that orthopraxis is a recurring leitmotif of Schillebeeckx's theological hermeneutics. In his words:

> It is therefore clear that a theologically actualizing interpretation is not possible without a critical theory which acts as a self-consciousness of a critical praxis. If the unity of faith takes place in real history, in other words, if it is itself really history, then we must not hope to be able to attain unity in faith either purely hermeneutically or by means of a purely theoretical theological interpretation. History is a flesh and blood affair and what has come about in history . . . can never be put right by purely theoretical means.[51]

As is clearly evident, Schillebeeckx's transformation, on account of his contextual influences, shaped not only his personal life but his theological thought as well. Having begun in the neo-scholastic tradition, the same tradition employed by the Vatican declaration *Dominus Iesus*, he then underwent a conversion upon his encounter with, literally, the larger world. The challenge posed by secularism as well as alternative forms of spirituality, and his engagement with philosophical hermeneutics as well as critical theory, led him to develop the hermeneutical-critical method of doing theology as a Catholic theologian. This, it must be added, was something very new within Roman Catholic circles in the 1960s. Suffice to say that since then many others have also followed in his footsteps, including and especially Asian theologians engaging in interreligious dialogue.

The next chapter will look at the essential elements or fruits of Schillebeeckx's theology as developed in accordance with the principles of the new theological methodology he espoused. Its focus will be on how this method enables him to address the theological concerns raised by the Vatican document *Dominus Iesus*.

---

50. Schillebeeckx, "Church as Sacrament," 136.
51. Schillebeeckx, *Understanding of Faith*, 132.

5

Schillebeeckx's Trilogy: Theology of *Dominus Iesus*

ONE OF THE FIRST results of Schillebeeckx's theological transformation and adoption of the hermeneutical-critical method of doing theology was explicated in his monumental works on Christology, which was to later appear in three volumes. This trilogy, sometimes referred to as his christological tome, is at once a theology in response to the circumstances surrounding the Church as well as those surrounding the increasingly postmodern and post-religious world.

It comes as no surprise then that just before that, an earlier first fruit of Schillebeeckx's late 60s–early 70s personal formation was a 1972 article entitled "Access to Jesus of Nazareth." The article not only traces the two "quests for the historical Jesus" but also distinguishes between the historical Jesus (that which can be reconstructed by historical studies) and the earthly or natural Jesus (the real person of Jesus of Nazareth). These themes, and much more, were to be systematically elaborated upon in his christological trilogy. These were the three books that brought Schillebeeckx to greater prominence as a systematic theologian not only in Europe but in the entire world as well.

THE CHRISTOLOGICAL TRILOGY

The first to constitute this trilogy is the mammoth book *Jesus*, published in 1974. The second volume appeared a few years later, in 1977, the English title of which is *Christ*. More than a decade later, in 1989, the third and final part of the trilogy appeared and was published in English as *Church*. While each of these books looks at different aspects of systematic theology, they are also often regarded as progressions of Schillebeeckx's christological research and so could all be classified under the one theme of the "Jesus books."

Jesus

The first Jesus book, published in 1974, was entitled in Dutch *Jezus, het verhaal van een levende*, which translates literally as "Jesus, the Story of the Living One." The English translation, published in 1979, was entitled *Jesus: An Experiment in Christology*. Hailed as "Schillebeeckx's lifework," it was truly a manifestation of his years of study, especially in the fields of historical-criticism, biblical exegesis, hermeneutics, and critical theory. The main focus of the book is Jesus, the human person who walked the streets of Nazareth two thousand years ago. Hence, *Jesus* was really an investigation of Jesus "from below," and not one that took for granted the dogmatic and ontological claims "from above."

This is because Schillebeeckx's aim in writing the book was not so much to verify or contest Church doctrines—as was often done in academic theology—but to "bridge the gap between academic theology and the concrete needs of the ordinary Christian."[1] He was responding to the urgent questions raised by contemporary Christians whose interest is in how Christian beliefs—in the time of the early Christians and for the Christian of today—came into being. The Christian is curious as to why is it that Jesus has such a following with his effect lasting two millennia, but not John the Baptist or Spartacus. The Christian is also curious as to what Jesus meant to the early disciples and who he is to the disciple of today. The Christian today is, therefore, similarly confronted with Jesus's question to his early disciples, "But who do you say that I am?" (Mark 8:29).

In *Jesus* Schillebeeckx uses modern biblical scholarship to unveil the life of Jesus as well as the response of the early Christians in such a way that the contemporary Christian recognizes that the story of Jesus is actually the story of God. In Jesus's life, teachings, and praxis the concerns of the Christian (then and now) are seen as the concerns of God. The human being's concerns are Jesus's concerns, as are God's concerns. The story of Jesus is, therefore, at once the story of the human being Jesus of Nazareth and the story of God. This accounts for why the Dutch subtitle to the book means "the Story of the Living One."

---

1. Schillebeeckx, *Jesus*, v.

The book's principal thrust is to tell God's story in Jesus's story. It does this by reconstructing the origins of the Christian faith among the first disciples from the beginning of Jesus's ministry up until the time of the formation of the New Testament canon. It had to go behind and beyond the New Testament texts, specifically the Synoptics, to discern a portrait of Jesus and that of the Christian faith. It was a quest for the historical Jesus, but a quest with a difference. It differed from the liberal nineteenth-century quest in that whereas the liberal quest attempted to excavate an objective Jesus detached from the community and Christian faith, Schillebeeckx's attempt was to do the same but taking seriously the experiences of the first "Christian movement." Schillebeeckx's historical investigations were as concerned about Jesus as they were of the Christian movement, in so far as what the Christians believed pointed to what Jesus looked like.

The starting point of Schillebeeckx's historical-critical investigations is, in his own words, "the first Christian community—but as a reflection of what Jesus himself was, said and did."[2] Schillebeeckx, therefore, had a dual starting point, which could be expressed thus: "Via the reflex of Jesus in the local churches we do indeed reach the historical Jesus. In his disciples we may detect the Master."[3] This method is what Schillebeeckx regards as the "general correlation principle" in that "the community is [as much] a reflection of Jesus."[4] The experience of the Christian community is, therefore, crucial to Schillebeeckx's theological task.

In this regard, the christological dogmas were certainly not Schillebeeckx's starting point. At a later time he remarked that his intention had really been to "dissociate the story of Jesus from all that dogmatic theology and to go back to that man, Jesus of Nazareth, who appeared in that place and at that time."[5] Bowden even suggests that Schillebeeckx's professed aim was to "free Jesus from dogmatics."[6] In this sense it is easy to understand why Schillebeeckx calls the first of his trilogy a "Jesus book." It simply means his focus was on the "down-to-earth" human Jesus and not so much the metaphysical God-man of dogmatic theology. On

2. Ibid., 44.
3. Ibid., 410.
4. Ibid., 427.
5. Schillebeeckx, *God Is New*, 20.
6. Bowden, *Edward Schillebeeckx*, 57.

the other hand Schillebeeckx was also quick to point out that the book did not altogether neglect the Christ of faith either.[7]

Christ

If the *Jesus* book did not neglect the Christ of faith, the *Christ* book did not neglect the Jesus of history either. The second volume of the trilogy takes for granted the findings of the first on the historical Jesus and proceeds to "the New Testament elaboration of what Christians experienced in their encounter with Jesus the Lord."[8] The original book was entitled *Gerechtigheid en liefde: Genade en bevrijding*, literally "Justice and Love: Grace and Liberation." The English translation was published as *Christ: The Christian Experience in the Modern World*. Following closely the Dutch title, *Christ* is a book on the early Church's understanding of grace and liberation, where the perspective taken is that of justice and love. Schillebeeckx explicates it thus: "In this book I want to analyze the New Testament experience of grace and salvation from God in Jesus Christ as an orientation for what we might call a first attempt at a modern Christian soteriology."[9] His concern was "with the question how *New Testament Christianity* experienced and analyzed salvation in and through Jesus, and with the question of the historical circumstances (then and now) through which this New Testament witness forms a normative orientation for our experience and interpretation of salvation in Jesus."[10]

Employing his exegetical skills Schillebeeckx pored through all the New Testament texts (save for the Synoptics, which he had already done when writing *Jesus*), with special focus on the Pauline and Johannine literature, to elucidate the theology of grace and salvation as experienced by the early Christian community. The *Christ* volume's concern is primarily with the New Testament texts as such. Schillebeeckx took "the texts seriously in their unity and as a whole . . . seeing them in their specific *literary* context against the background of the literature of the time, within the specific socio-cultural reality of the milieu above all of those for whom these New Testament texts were directly written."[11]

---

7. Schillebeeckx, *Jesus*, v.
8. Schillebeeckx, *Christ*, 22.
9. Ibid.
10. Ibid., 24.
11. Ibid., 23.

In so doing Schillebeeckx's method shifted from the use of historical-criticism, and the concomitant form and redaction criticisms, to the use of literary criticism in order to read and understand the texts "as they are." At the same time, in keeping with the hermeneutical principle of correlation between Christian tradition and present experience, Schillebeeckx takes note of how—"then and now"—Christians understand and experience salvation in a pluralistic way. Just as the New Testament depicts numerous ways of understanding what salvation is from and what salvation is for—"from what and for what are we freed?"[12]—contemporary Christians also understand salvation in a variety of ways. In the spirit of the understanding of the early Christians, Schillebeeckx contends that the present Christian's belief in the pluralism of salvation is not only allowed but acknowledged as biblically sound.

Church

The issue of pluralism was elaborated upon in the third volume of the trilogy, *Church*. Schillebeeckx describes the book in the foreword as an examination of the life of Christians in the context of religious pluralism: "This book is about the life of men and women and their bond with God as God has become visible above all in Jesus of Nazareth, confessed as the Christ by the Christian churches—which are increasingly aware that they live in a secular world amidst other religions."[13] Originally intended as an ecclesiological third part of the trilogy, the book's Dutch title reads *Mensen als verhaal van God*, literally "Human Beings as God's Story." The English version was later published as *Church: The Human Story of God*.

However, in view of the developments within Roman Catholicism in the period since *Christ*—one might recall here the conflicts within the Dutch Church and its conflicts with Rome, as well as Schillebeeckx's own personal conflicts with Curial officials and the CDF's 1980s crusade on liberation theologies and other efforts of Church renewal—Schillebeeckx had this to say: "Delight in belonging to this church, a delight which increased greatly during the Second Vatican Council and the years immediately following, has been sorely tested over the last decade." Schillebeeckx added that he no longer felt enthused about writing a book on the Church, lest his energies be drawn into examining the secondary "domestic church

12. Ibid., 477–514.
13. Schillebeeckx, *Church*, xiii.

problems" rather than exploring the more essential thrusts, viz., "what Christians should be doing in this world."[14]

It makes sense therefore that Schillebeeckx focused his research on the external ministry of the Church rather than on its internal concerns. As such, the book *Church* turned out to be more an ecclesiology *ad extra* rather than an ecclesiology *ad intra*. It addresses issues of fundamental theology as diverse as history, salvation, revelation, religious experience, and suffering, as well as God, religion, faith, human existence, secularism, and mysticism. Only after exploring all these does it address issues of Christology and ecclesiology per se. It is important to note that Schillebeeckx explores the various topics in the context of "the heart of the gospel and the Christian religion, [especially] its distinctive and unique features."[15] *Church* looks at the essence of Christianity or what it means to be Christian and Church in an increasingly secular and pluralistic world. It does this by expanding the Church's horizons so that Christians see their mission as in the world rather than for the Church. Beginning *Church* with a chapter entitled "A Guide to the Book," Schillebeeckx turns the old adage *extra ecclesiam nulla salus*—"outside the Church there is no salvation"—to *extra mundum nulla salus*—"outside the world there is no salvation."[16] In *Church* Schillebeeckx puts the Church "in its place" while at the same time also giving the Church "the place which is its due."

Church was some sort of synthesis of Schillebeeckx's entire trilogy in that it repeats much of what was in the first two volumes but in the context of the late 1980s, with increasing Church centralization, the rise of Islam, the fall of the USSR and the resultant chaos in Eastern Europe, and an acceleration in the process of secularization.[17] *Church*, therefore, has to be read in concert with *Christ* and *Jesus*.

SCHILLEBEECKX'S THEOLOGY OF DOMINUS IESUS

The thrust of Schillebeeckx's reflection in the three volumes is on what it means to continue believing in Jesus Christ in a world beset with destruction, despair, and disbelief. It was Schillebeeckx's way of offering "Jesus as Lord" to the late-twentieth-century Christian. This next section will

14. Ibid.
15. Ibid.
16. Ibid., xvii.
17. Ibid., 229.

offer a cursory view of Schillebeeckx's trilogy, with reference especially to the issues raised by the CDF's *Dominus Iesus*. Of significance is how Schillebeeckx addresses the issues of revelation, salvation, the uniqueness of Christ and of the Church, and the relation of Christianity to other religions.

As is evident, the central questions of one's faith have all been addressed in the three volumes of *Jesus*, *Christ*, and *Church*. In each volume Schillebeeckx explores the issues pertaining to specific questions: "Who do you say that I am?" was addressed in the *Jesus* book; "What does salvation from God in Jesus mean to us?" was addressed in the *Christ* book; and "What is the Church's response to this offer of salvation?" was addressed in the *Church* book. These are questions centered upon the foundation of one's faith. They are questions as relevant to the early Christians as they are to contemporary Christians.

They are also the very same questions raised by the Vatican's 2000 declaration *Dominus Iesus*, even if phrased differently. The declaration's concerns are as follows: How do we understand revelation and salvation? How do we understand the uniqueness and universality of Jesus Christ and of the Church? What is the relationship between the Kingdom of God and the Church? What is the place of other religions in God's plan of salvation? How do we respond to the threat of relativism and religious pluralism? How do we understand the mission of the Church? And finally, how do we go about in interreligious dialogue? In sum, these questions in *Dominus Iesus* ask about Jesus Christ's identity, which is a christological question (who do you say that I am?), his salvific value, which is a soteriological question (what does salvation in Jesus mean?), and the Church's mission and relation to the world and to other religions, which is an ecclesiological question (what is the Church's response to the world?).

One could even say that in the trilogy Schillebeeckx had more or less anticipated the questions raised by *Dominus Iesus*, or that the trilogy constitutes his response to the concerns raised by the document. The trilogy could even be regarded as Schillebeeckx's own proclamation of *Dominus Iesus* in that it is "an offer" of a Christian confession of faith that "Jesus is Lord." This will be explored below. But since the aim is to compare Schillebeeckx's theology and approach with that of the Vatican's, only aspects of his theology that relate to *Dominus Iesus* will be looked at. Inasmuch as they are issues raised by *Dominus Iesus* they will be examined, for it is certainly impossible for the trilogy, which counts about two thousand pages, to be condensed into several pages.[18] At best, the central theses of Schillebeeckx's theology will be enumerated.

A creed at the very end of *Christ* is used to provide some sort of framework to accomplish this. This creed was a personal adaptation and expansion by Schillebeeckx of a composition of the poet Michel van der Plas based on the earliest Christian creeds. Schillebeeckx situates it at the end of the *Christ* book as, in his own words, an "affirmative confession of what God himself has given us."[19] Again, it represents Schillebeeckx's own personal confession of the Christian faith. The theology of Schillebeeckx's faith, which is capsulized in this tripartite creed, will be examined in the ensuing reflections through the tripartite structure that follows.

"I Believe in God, the Father"

> I believe in God, the Father: the omnipotence of love.
> He is the Creator of heaven and earth;
> this whole universe, with all its mysteries;
> this earth on which we live, and the stars to which we travel.
> He knows us from eternity, he never forgets
> that we are made of the dust of the earth
> and that one day we shall return again to it as dust.[20]

To begin, Schillebeeckx speaks of God as "essentially creator, the lover of the finite, loving with the absoluteness of a divine love which is unfathomable to us."[21] His reflections give primacy to the notion of God as the one who created the world. This theme of God as creator of heaven and earth occupies a foundational role in Schillebeeckx's theology. He has often remarked that the doctrine of creation is the "foundation of all theology"[22] and that a "creation faith" is the "background and horizon of all Christian belief."[23]

---

18. In addition to the three volumes, a very small book entitled *Interim Report* is also part of the Jesus corpus. It was written by Schillebeeckx to clarify the many questions and criticisms raised by the first two books, as well as questions raised during the Vatican's investigations of him.

19. Schillebeeckx, *Christ*, 846.

20. Ibid., 847.

21. Ibid., 181.

22. Schillebeeckx, *Happy Theologian*, 47.

23. Schillebeeckx, *Church*, 90.

This doctrine is rooted in the Pentateuch's understanding of God, as depicted by "the Exodus name of God, 'I AM WHO I AM' (Exod 3:14)," which, Schillebeeckx explains, is in reference to Yahweh saying "I am there for man as king (*hanan*), and also as mother and father (*raham*)."[24] *Hanan* here refers to the graciousness of God while *raham* to God's mercy. Thus, Yahweh Lord is "a God merciful and gracious, slow to anger, and abounding in steadfast love and faithfulness" (Exod 34: 6). It follows that this God who is gracious and merciful cannot but want to freely share God's love in creation. Creation is but an act of love on God's part and, more importantly, "an act of God's trust in man."[25]

The sort of trust referred to by the Yahwist in the book of Exodus is likened to the trust between God and King David as depicted in the Yahwist royal theology: "David, 'the small man,' 'taken from behind the sheep' (2 Sam 7:18b; 7:8c), 'exalted out of the dust' (1 Kgs 16:1–3; see 1 Sam 2:6–8; Ps 113:7; Gen 2:7), who is not worthy of trust in himself, is taken from the dust, and made the subject of God's unconditional trust (1 Sam 7:8–12): he is raised to be king from the dust, or from nothing at all."[26] The divine trust is an unconditional free gift—much like God's trust in David—offered to "Adam," or all of humankind, for no reason other than because God chooses to trust in creation. In response, just as David's role and duty was to reciprocate this divine trust by acting justly and responsibly as king of his people, the human person's role and duty is likewise to be responsible for and in the service of the world and the rest of humanity. The sense of "co-humanity" is, therefore, an inherent virtue in our being creatures of the divine God.[27] It is a sense where humans care about humans and every person will be responsible for everyone else. But, just as Adam—as did David—fell and acted irresponsibly in the discharge of his duty, humankind is also liable—indeed, prone—to fall and to fail. As a result, they are punished, but with a punishment that does not seem to be commensurate with the gravity of the failure. God remains merciful and gracious and continues to manifest God's presence and omnipotent love unto the world and humankind despite human frailty and failings.

---

24. Ibid.
25. Schillebeeckx, *Interim*, 106.
26. Ibid., 108.
27. Schillebeeckx, *Church*, 236.

Such is the nature of God and, more importantly, such is the nature of humankind.

The doctrine of creation, therefore, is really a doctrine about God and the human being and especially about God's relationship with the world and with human beings. It is more a theological anthropology than a cosmology or any scientific theory on the physical constitution of the universe. The doctrine tells us who we are and how we ought to relate to one another and to God. Schillebeeckx points out that the "mythically developed story" of the Pentateuch aims at showing that "this is the way in which God intended the ordering of the world and this is how it must remain, i.e., as a world in which all individuals and peoples live together in peace, each in their own territory, even in cosmic peace in which human beings live as tenant farmers 'on the land flowing with milk and honey,' where the creator is constantly praised liturgically."[28] The stories of creation are principally aimed at recounting God's dealings and relationship with humankind, as well as recommending humanity's appropriate response to God.

It can be said that the doctrine of creation is founded upon the ideal that human beings must be in relationship with God, as well as in relationship with one another and with all other living beings and the rest of nature. Such is the foundation to understanding all of life and life's relationships. Thus, for example, when Gen 1:28 speaks of human beings as having "dominion over the fish of the sea and over the birds of the air and over every living thing that moves upon the earth," the word used, *radah*, is given to mean that "human beings must be friendly to other living beings."[29] Dominion, or to "rule over," is by no means a license to subjugate or to exploit but refers to the human being's role as guardian, leader, guide, and shepherd of all other living beings. Similarly, all other biblical accounts have to be understood in such a context of love and relationship.

Essentially, the doctrine of creation teaches that "God is God, the sun is the sun, the moon is the moon and man is man."[30] It's as simple as that. Each has its own place and each has its own particular nature. As creator, God creates only that which is "not divine" and "not God." In

---

28. Ibid., 242.
29. Ibid., 243.
30. Schillebeeckx, *Interim*, 113.

other words, all of creation is "not-God." If it were not "not-God," then it would be God and not a creation. It follows that all creation is by nature not perfect, not omnipotent, not infinite, not immortal, and not absolute. To be sure, creation is imperfect, finite, contingent, mortal, and unpredictable. Creation is, therefore, subject to making mistakes, being weak, and even to committing sinful and evil acts. It is not necessarily subject only to events and phenomena that have rational explanations, nor is it necessarily subject to the laws of teleology. Such is the condition of what it means to be created, a condition of finitude. God created in absolute freedom a creation whose nature is just not like God. These are all part of the "mysteries" of the universe that Schillebeeckx speaks about in his creed above.

Creation is even allowed to be as it pleases, without intervention from God. Schillebeeckx at times also speaks of the "impotence of God," an impotence willed freely by God.[31] God is not necessarily in charge of or in control of everything in the universe, nor does God want to be. The world and humanity cannot expect God to come to the rescue at all times and in all circumstances. They certainly cannot expect God to save them from finitude or from all that finitude entails. That is not what salvation is about. God created the world in such a way that the world will never be able to be "not-finite." It is in the nature of the world to be finite and thus imperfect. This is simply part of the trust that God has in creation. It is a sort of "divine yielding,"[32] where God makes room for creation to exist in total freedom, for the world to be as it pleases. In short, Schillebeeckx believes, God has freely willed to have no control over creation.

The transformation of the world and the planning for a better society are all in the hands of finite men and women who are free to develop the world as they see fit, except that these have to be within the confines of the limitation of finitude. Human beings, having free will and the freedom of choice, can choose between a variety of alternatives, except that these must be within the bounds of finitude—as metaphorically represented in Genesis by Adam not being permitted to eat of the tree of the knowledge of good and evil. Finitude is thus the nature of things and of the world. This finitude is looked upon as an intrinsic merit and essential goodness

---

31. Ibid., 115.
32. Schillebeeckx, *Church*, 90.

and not so much as some kind of flaw or shortcoming. Schillebeeckx speaks of it as "the worth of limitation."[33]

It would be a "mistake," therefore, if "finitude is regarded as a wound, something which need not really have been."[34] Such mistaken ideologies are wont to attribute finitude to some other cause or demonic power or to regard it as a result of some primal sin. Such ideologies do not accept finitude as part of the nature of the world and of history but as something that is improper and ought to be overcome. This lends itself to the view that contingency, imperfection, and sin are not supposed to exist and that perhaps human beings ought to have been infinite or infinitely perfect. Such would have been the case, it is thought, if not for the fact that these infinite attributes were lost or taken away as a result of some original sin or first fall. The book of Job clearly testifies against such views. Other parts of the Bible are also clearly against such views, as represented by the Genesis accounts of the eating of the fruit and the story of the tower of Babel. A desire to be like God and wanting to transcend the finitude and contingency of life "is arrogance which alienates man from himself, the world and nature."[35] Schillebeeckx regards such desires as the "fundamental human sin" as they are attempts to challenge God's creation by disowning one's human nature. Unfortunately, it is a sin repeated over and over throughout the course of human history, even until today.

While on the one hand there is the recognition of the finitude of humanity, on the other hand there is also the affirmation of the infinity of God, the transcendent reality. These are two sides of the same coin. Limitation and contingency are the very elements that distinguish the creator God from created beings. This creator, the God of omnipotent love and absolute presence, manifests the attributes of God within the finite. Belief in the creator God situates the human being within a condition of limitation and finitude as well as within the presence of God's absolute grace and mercy. This is not to imply that God will remove our finitude since our finitude can always be taken up into the presence of God who is gracious and merciful.

A Christian's "creation faith," therefore, implies a belief in a God who is boundless in "omnipotent love" and who loved us "for nothing." This is

---

33. Kennedy, *Schillebeeckx*, 86.
34. Schillebeeckx, *Interim*, 113.
35. Ibid., 114.

expressed in Paul as "God proves his love for us in that while we still were sinners Christ died for us" (Rom 5:8) and in John as "In this is love, not that we loved God but that he loved us and sent his Son to be the atoning sacrifice for our sins" (1 John 4:10). Such is the "selfless love" of God who is at once the "supreme content" as well as the "deepest meaning" of what it means to be truly human. The creator God is the principle and goal of humanity and represents its salvation and happiness.[36] God is one who "knows us from all eternity" and who "never forgets," as well as one who inspires life and goodness but always respecting the finitude of human nature.

Salvation, therefore, is not about God saving us from finitude or from the world of contingency, but about God providing the strength and inspiration that will help us to lift ourselves up from the evil and suffering that so pervades the world. The doctrine of creation is, therefore, at once the doctrine of salvation. God's creation is the beginning of the history of salvation just as the whole of creation is permeated with God's saving intent. God is and has always been there, in the "dust of the earth" and in our suffering and failures. God is and has always been there, in the "stars to which we travel" and in our prosperity and successes. God is ever ready to give hope and to lend a hand, to forgive and to heal, and to finally offer God's salvation so that we shall one day "return again to God as dust." Such is the "creation faith" that Schillebeeckx's theology speaks about, and such is the hope this faith engenders.

By whose authority are the foregoing reflections about creation and salvation based upon? Who told us so and how did we arrive at such knowledge? Schillebeeckx posits that it is our human experience that is the basis of such reflections. He is emphatic that theological reflections ought to come only after the fact of our experience. Within the context of "creation faith," it has been our human experience that revealed to us that such is the nature of salvation. We know it because we experience it as such in discerning the events of history and in reflecting on our present-day realities. Our theological reflections are derived from these lived experiences of what salvation is like for us.

But then, how do we know what salvation is supposed to be? How do we know that goodness is our final destiny and evil is bad? On the basis of our experience alone we do not know for sure. Responding to these

36. Ibid., 126.

questions Schillebeeckx suggests that we do have a "faint idea" of what salvation is like as reflected "through human experiences of goodness, meaning and love" and through situations where we "experience a threat to what is human in us."[37] The fact that we rejoice and look forward to the former and rebel against and reject the latter gives us an indication as to what our true human nature is supposed to be. This seems to be the inherent knowledge of good and evil that we derive from our own lived experience. But as Christians we do have another clue, which we shall explore below.

"I Believe in Jesus Christ"

> I believe in Jesus Christ, the only-beloved Son of God.
> For love of all of us, he has willed to share our history, our existence with us.
> I believe that God also wanted to be our God in a human way.
> He has dwelt as man among us, a light in the darkness.
> But the darkness did not overcome him.
> We nailed him to the cross.
> And he died and was buried.
> But he trusted in God's final word, and is risen, once and for all;
> he said that he would prepare a place for us,
> in his Father's house, where he now dwells.[38]

Our experience of creation and salvation is also verified and given definitive form in the person of Jesus of Nazareth, who through his life revealed to us "everything that is good in creation."[39] This, according to Schillebeeckx, is because Jesus is "the ultimate key to understanding human existence" as in his life one sees "the final promise of God's unconditional trust in mankind and the perfect human response to this divine trust."[40] It is in this sense that the Christian belief in the creator God is essentially bound to the belief in the person of Jesus as God's definitive salvation.

Jesus amplifies clearly the "meaning of creation as the manifestation of God's nature, as the beginning of salvation, and, in biblical categories,

---

37. Ibid., 130.
38. Schillebeeckx, *Christ*, 847.
39. Kennedy, *Schillebeeckx*, 94.
40. Schillebeeckx, *Interim*, 109.

as the inauguration of God's kingdom."[41] In Jesus, God's trust in humanity through creation was "not put to shame." Schillebeeckx speaks of Jesus as "concentrated creation, . . . the man in whom the task of creation has been successfully accomplished."[42] It has to be pointed out that this is not so much that the belief in the God of creation precedes the belief in Jesus as it is that the two beliefs mutually interpret and reinforce one another. In other words, the doctrine of creation sheds light on Jesus's life just as Jesus's life clarifies the doctrine of creation.

Thus, over and above our own experience of what salvation is like, the life and teachings of Jesus of Nazareth also reveal aspects about God and about salvation that we may never know by ourselves from our own lived experience. It is through how the human Jesus lived his life and the message that he preached, as well as through the circumstances surrounding his death and the apostolic witness of his resurrection, that we know God as "liberating love for humanity, in a way which fulfils and transcends all human, personal, social and political expectations."[43] That Jesus is the Christ, the Son of God, and the definitive revelation from God for our salvation is the testimony of Christians.

Christians see in Jesus who is "personally human" God sharing in human history. Jesus is God being God in a human way in order to dwell among us as a human being. In the person of Jesus the kingdom of God comes very close to us since the kingdom is essentially connected with the person of Jesus of Nazareth.[44] It is in this context that Schillebeeckx speaks of Jesus as "parable of God and paradigm of humanity."[45] In Jesus God's love story with humankind is told just as humanity's obedient and love response to God is recounted. Johannine theology has it that "whoever does not love does not know God, for God is love. God's love was revealed among us in this way: God sent his only Son into the world so that we might live through him" (1 John 4:8–9).

In order to better understand the meaning of salvation from God it is important that we first appreciate the life, teaching, and witness of Jesus who was "personally human." In this regard Schillebeeckx points out that

41. Ibid.
42. Ibid., 111.
43. Ibid., 128.
44. Schillebeeckx, *Church*, 112.
45. Schillebeeckx, *Jesus*, 626ff.

there is no mention of the message and life of Jesus in the traditional Christian creed. From the article "born of the virgin Mary" the creed takes us immediately to "suffered under Pontius Pilate," significantly bypassing the entire life and ministry of Jesus. How then can we understand and appreciate the life and witness of Jesus through a meditation on the Christian creed? Schillebeeckx sees this as a significant part of the Christian tradition and suggests that the creed is but a résumé of the person of Jesus and so cannot stand alone but has to be taken in concert with the witness of the Gospels.[46] The portrait of the human Jesus as depicted in the New Testament is an essential supplement to the Christian creed in our understanding of God's offer of salvation in Jesus Christ. Any understanding of the Christian faith, therefore, has to take seriously the story of Jesus as given to us in the Gospels.

To begin with, the Gospels regard the "kingdom of God" as central to the entire life and preaching of Jesus. Also called "God's reign," "rule of God," or "*basileia tou Theou*," it refers to God's "unconditional and liberating sovereign love, in so far as this comes into being and reveals itself in the life of men and women who do God's will."[47] Schillebeeckx defines this kingdom as both "already" and "not yet," in that it is already experienced in the here and now, as well as something that awaits fulfillment. Where "men and women encounter Jesus in faith, the sick are healed, demons are driven out, sinners are led to repentance and the poor discover their worth . . . the kingdom of God is experienced here and now both by Jesus and the one who encountered him."[48] On the other hand, "the kingdom of God is [also] an eschatological event, still to come (Mark 14:25; Luke 22:15–18): the eschatological feast lies in the future; Jesus participates in it with his disciples."[49] The whole of Jesus's message and praxis was about actualizing the kingdom of God, "with the emphasis at once on its coming and on its coming close."[50] The Gospel imperative that we "strive first for the kingdom of God and his righteousness, and all these things will be given to you" (Matt 6:33) at once guides our exploration into the meaning of Jesus as does how Christian living is to be lived to its fullest.

46. Schillebeeckx, *Interim*, 129.
47. Schillebeeckx, *Church*, 111.
48. Ibid., 132–33.
49. Schillebeeckx, *Jesus*, 150.
50. Ibid., 140.

The "already" and "not yet" of the kingdom are linked, just as Jesus's proclamation of the kingdom and the conduct of his life are linked. They are related in such a way that the kingdom is already made present in Jesus's earthly life and that his earthly ministry is about actualizing the kingdom. Significantly, the coming of God's kingdom entails a *metanoia* on our part. This, Schillebeeckx asserts, is expressed in nothing less than a conversion to the actual praxis of the kingdom of God. This is the basis to why in the Lord's Prayer the clause "your kingdom come" is immediately followed by "your will be done on earth." It suggests the imperative of orthopraxis or right conduct for God's reign to come.[51] The New Testament speaks not only of Jesus's teaching and proclamation but also of his associating with sinners, giving sight to the blind, healing the lame, associating with women and taking the side of the outcasts and the marginalized. In short, Jesus "went about doing good" (Acts 10:38), as "doing good" is God's cause just as it is the human's cause. All of Jesus's activities—his miracles of healing and driving out of demons, his presence with the people, his offering and accepting invitations to table fellowship, not just with his disciples but also with the publicans, the sinners, and the outcasts—point to the offer of God's salvation and relationship with humankind: "the intercourse of Jesus of Nazareth with his fellow-men is an offer of salvation-imparted-by-God; it has to do with the coming rule of God, as proclaimed by him."[52]

The connection between this orthopraxis and the reign of God is clearly evidenced in the many parables told by Jesus. As narratives with a twist, the parables are intended to startle and to jolt as they invite the hearer to review her/his life so as to look at it from another angle, perhaps God's angle. Parables have a practical and critical effect in that they "open up new and different potentialities for living, often in contrast with our conventional ways of behaving."[53] For example, through the parables of the lost son (Luke 15:11–32), lost coin (Luke 15:8–10), and lost sheep (Matt 18:12–14; Luke 15:4–7) God's gracious love especially for the lost and the marginalized are brought to prominence. Through the parable of the Pharisee and the publican or tax collector (Luke 18:10–14) "the pious Pharisee who in fact keeps the law scrupu-

---

51. Ibid., 152–53.
52. Ibid., 179.
53. Ibid., 157.

lously and thanks God because he is not like this sinner is turned away by God, [while] the publican who feels unworthy to appear before God goes away 'justified.'"[54] Through the parable of the workers in the vineyard (Matt 20:1–16) "Jesus presents a very provocative picture of God: God remains free in handing out his gifts and favors."[55] Schillebeeckx ultimately postulates Jesus himself as the "parable of God."[56] By this he refers to the ever unconventional and incomprehensible person of Jesus, his praxis and proclamation, characterized by "the 'shock' effect [which] marks the ongoing sequence of his life."[57]

Through the parables and Jesus's praxis of the kingdom it seems clear that the kingdom of God is a totally new order of a relationship between God and humanity and between humanity themselves. It is new in that it is an utterly liberating and reconciling message but at the same time not in conformity with norms of the regular social order. The *basileia tou Theou* "does not know the human logic of precise justice. Jesus wants to give hope to those who from a social and human point of view, according to our human rules, no longer have any hope."[58] The only logic for Jesus, according to Schillebeeckx, is that the kingdom is essentially directed to the uplifting of the poor and the outcast. This logic represents the principal criterion by which God's kingdom is discerned: "Jesus' picture of God is determined by the thirsty, the stranger, the prisoner, the sick, the outcast; here he sees God (Matt 25)." Likewise, Jesus's actions and teachings are directed towards actualizing the picture of the world that God wills. In Jesus's actions one sees how God would act: "So in him there is a claim that God himself is present in his actions and words. To act as Jesus does is praxis of the kingdom of God, and moreover a demonstration of what the kingdom of God is: salvation for men and women."[59]

Throughout the trilogy Schillebeeckx speaks of Jesus as the "eschatological prophet," the "final prophet-greater-than-Moses."[60] This is the "matrix which gave rise to four pre–New Testament credal models which

---

54. Schillebeeckx, *Church*, 115.
55. Ibid.
56. Ibid., 156.
57. Ibid., 157.
58. Ibid., 117.
59. Ibid., 118.
60. Schillebeeckx, *Jesus*, 476ff; *Christ*, 312ff.

later [came] together in the New Testament under the all-embracing title of Easter Christology."[61] Each of the four creedal models emphasizes a particular historical aspect of Jesus's life: the *maranatha* Christology emphasizes the coming of Jesus as the eschatological Lord of the end times, the Parousia; the *theios aner* Christology presents Jesus in the power mode, as divine miracle-worker; the *wisdom* Christology speaks of Jesus as the pre-existent Wisdom, incarnate and intermediary between God and humanity; the *Easter* Christology proclaims the salvific death of Jesus as the crucified-and-risen one. The "eschatological prophet" title integrates these four strands together so that the phenomenon of Jesus is "corrected and filled out by one another" to culminate "within the one fundamental vision of the crucified and risen Jesus" as seen in the Gospels and the New Testament.[62]

Schillebeeckx further posits that the "source and secret" of Jesus's "being, message and manner of life" lies in his original *Abba* experience.[63] Jesus's self-understanding as the eschatological prophet is shaped primarily by his intimate relationship with God whom he addressed by the familial term *Abba*. This is a break from the Judaic norms of his time, which placed a distance between God and humanity. In his *Abba* experience Jesus makes the point that God can be approached in a personal way, much the same way someone approaches his/her own "daddy." It is at once an experience of "unaffected and natural simplicity"[64] as it is an experience of total obedience and submission to God: "Not my will, but your will, Father" (Luke 21:42; Matt 26:42).

All of the above have to be understood in the context of Jesus's final days on earth, especially his passion, death, and subsequent resurrection. Of significance is that this fateful end to the person of Jesus came about as a direct consequence of his ministry, his message, and above all his praxis. Specifically, it was the Sanhedrin—mainly the Sadducees and not so much the Pharisees—who condemned Jesus: "Jesus was condemned as a pseudo-teacher (deceiver of the people) on the basis of Deut 17:12," pointing to Jesus's religious activities as the source of his conflict with the Jewish ruling class.[65] However, "owing to the political implications of his

61. Schillebeeckx, *Interim*, 69.
62. Ibid., 70.
63. Schillebeeckx, *Jesus*, 256–71.
64. Ibid., 261.
65. Ibid., 313.

public activity." Jesus was then handed over to the Romans.[66] Indeed, his being "crucified under Pontius Pilate" is significant as it was "the great historical testimony that the message of Jesus actually had a politically dangerous side."[67] Thus, it was his career, specifically his religious and political activities, that brought Jesus to his death. It was not so much that God had sent Jesus to be crucified but human beings who put him to the death, in particular those whose status and powers were threatened by Jesus's proclamation and praxis. Schillebeeckx contends that "Jesus was indeed condemned because he remained true to his prophetic mission 'from God,' a mission which he refused to justify to any other authority than God himself."[68] For Jesus, God's cause was so important that he even "thought his life to be of less value than the cause for which he stood: the coming of God's kingdom as salvation from man for man."[69] His death is not a death "overcome by darkness." Even if nailed to the cross, Jesus continued to "trust in God's final word." It is such that Jesus's death cannot stand alone, lest it be no more than that of a failed messiah on a failed mission. It has to be interpreted in light of the resurrection.

At the outset Schillebeeckx distinguishes between the resurrection, which is a non-empirical and trans-historical event, and belief in Jesus's resurrection, which is "an event of and in our history, and as such is in principle accessible to a historical and genetic analysis."[70] The resurrection faith is by no means founded upon the narratives of the empty tomb or Jesus's appearances. It precedes these traditions. Belief in the resurrection began with "a process of conversion, from disenchantment with Jesus to *metanoia*."[71] Schillebeeckx posits that this conversion among the disciples took place even before Jesus's death, as represented by Peter who broke down and wept in remorse for his earlier denial of Jesus (Mark 14:72). With the crucifixion of Jesus, Peter—as did the other disciples—called to mind Jesus's earthly ministry and particularly his message of a merciful God of salvation. They experienced a renewal and subsequently proclaimed Jesus as "the eschatological prophet, the one who is to come,

66. Ibid., 317.
67. Schillebeeckx, *Interim*, 133.
68. Schillebeeckx, *Jesus*, 317.
69. Schillebeeckx, *Interim*, 142.
70. Ibid., 75.
71. Ibid., 77.

the redeemer of the world, the Christ, the Son of Man and the Son of God."[72] Like Jesus, Peter too "trusted in God's final word" and so was able to proclaim Jesus as "risen, once and for all." It is this same trust that enables us to believe that Jesus "would prepare a place for us, in his Father's house, where he now dwells."

For Schillebeeckx, there is "no gap between Jesus' self-understanding and the Christ proclaimed by the Church."[73] Hence, his resurrection is a vindication of his murder in the hands of the ruling elites. Likewise, the resurrection also validates Jesus's entire ministry of proclamation and praxis. In fact, the whole of Jesus's life can be seen as mutually interpreting and reinforcing God's salvific grace of creation. Similarly, the actions of the creator God and Jesus, the Christ, the Son of God, can only be understood more fully in light of the subsequent mission of Jesus's disciples, the Church, acting through God the Holy Spirit.

"I Believe in the Holy Spirit"

> I believe in the Holy Spirit, who is the Lord and gives life.
> And for the prophets among us, he is language, power and fire.
> I believe that together we are all on a journey, pilgrims,
> called and gathered together, to be God's holy people,
> for I confess freedom from evil,
> the task of bringing justice and the courage to love.
> I believe in eternal life, in love that is stronger than death,
> in a new heaven and a new earth.
> And I believe that I may hope for a life with God and with one another for all eternity:
> Glory for God and peace for men.[74]

From the outset Schillebeeckx asserts that religions and Churches are sacraments of God's salvation in the world. While they do not bring about salvation, they serve as signs of God's offer of salvation. In other words, God's offer of salvation is indeed effected in the community through the ministries of the various Churches and religions. This is in keeping with Schillebeeckx's thesis of *extra mundum nulla salus*, which assumes that salvation is achieved in and through the world wherein "the religions are

---

72. Ibid.
73. Schillebeeckx, *Jesus*, 312.
74. Schillebeeckx, *Christ*, 847–48.

the place where men and women become explicitly aware of God's saving actions in history."[75] The religions and churches are the sacraments of salvation as they are "the *anamnesis*, i.e., the living recollection among us, of this universal, 'tacit' but effective will to salvation and the absolute saving presence of God in our world history."[76] Schillebeeckx is explicit that religions other than Christianity are as much vehicles of God's salvific acts and "ways of salvation." He points to Vatican II's *Nostra Aetate*, which reminds us that men and women look to different religions for the "message of salvation and the opening of a way of salvation."[77] It follows that persons who belong to religions other than Christianity find salvation not so much "despite" their religion but precisely "in" and "through" them.

This in no way suggests that Schillebeeckx lends himself to the thesis that "all religions are equal, equally relative, or equally wrong."[78] He strongly admonishes such perceptions, which he regards as a "particular new form of modern 'indifferentism.'"[79] Such indifferentism, rooted in the post-Enlightenment disdain for claims to truth and universality, is "basically wrong" and a "cheap form of tolerance." This is where, according to Schillebeeckx, it is important that the religions be a form of "criticism and provocation of this spirit of the time." They do so without tending towards the other extreme, which is that of absolutism. In other words, "we have to look in a direction in which both absolutism and relativism are avoided in connection with what is called 'religion.'"[80] Each religion has to allow itself to be "challenged by the other religions and which, on the basis of its own message, also challenges other religions."[81] No single religion—not even Christianity—can claim monopoly to nor exhaust the whole meaning of truth. God is the only absolute. As historical particularities, religions are relative in relation to God and to one another. They have to be brought into a critical correlation and confrontation with each other, so as to better discern truth from that which is untrue.

---

75. Schillebeeckx, *Church*, 12.
76. Ibid., 13.
77. Ibid., 160.
78. Ibid., 167.
79. Ibid., 162.
80. Ibid., 163.
81. Ibid., 164.

Hence, the question for us Christians is certainly not about whether Christianity is superior to other religions. Instead, "the question," according to Schillebeeckx, is "whether the pluralism of religions is a matter of fact or a matter of principle."[82] If religious pluralism is indeed a matter of principle the question then is not about Christianity being the one true religion. Instead, it is about how Christianity can "maintain its own identity and uniqueness and at the same time attach a positive value to the difference of religions in a non-discriminatory sense." Accordingly, "what is relevant to Christianity is not what is common to many religions, but precisely that difference between them which forms their uniqueness and distinctiveness." It is in view of this that Schillebeeckx deems it important that we explore anew Christianity's self-definition, including its claims to uniqueness and universality, as well as its foundation, which must lead to an "open and not-intolerant attitude" in order to put Christianity in its place while giving it its rightful place.[83]

Believing in God the Holy Spirit who is "the Lord who gives life" and who is the Spirit who wills that peoples of all religions are "together" as "pilgrims" and on "journey," Schillebeeckx posits that all religions are unique in and of themselves.[84] Each manifests a different face of God who is "ultimately the invisible and unnameable One." The "God who escapes all our identification" is "unimaginable" and "totally other even than as he has appeared in Jesus." That notwithstanding, Schillebeeckx posits that New Testament Christianity has stressed "the fact that God has shown us his face in the man Jesus." Christianity's distinctiveness is in identifying God, of which Jesus is its definition. The God of creation, who wills the salvation and love for all, is revealed in Jesus of Nazareth, the "historical, culturally located expression of this universal message of the gospel."[85]

It is noted that "this is a definition of God in non-divine terms, namely in and through the historical contingent humanity of Jesus."[86] Jesus's life and message as well as his passion and death by execution and his eventual resurrection by God, serve to provide the necessary clues to who God is and what God is like. Such an investigation into Jesus's life, besides

82. Ibid., 166.
83. Ibid., 165.
84. Ibid., 182.
85. Ibid., 179.
86. Ibid.

revealing who God is, also reveals what being human really means. The human person Jesus is the "God-given revelation of what 'being human' really implies and in and through that very fact there is disclosed what it means to 'be God.'"[87] In Jesus we have the norm and criterion of what it means to be human, as well as a disclosure into the being of God, the one who grants salvation to all. Schillebeeckx advocates that we "must simply try, through the New Testament, to discover how Jesus concretely lived out his being-as-man and how, for those who accepted him on trust, it became clear that people were able to encounter him in their experience as the savior of all men."[88] This accounts for why Schillebeeckx took so much time and trouble to discover who this Jesus the human being really was. It is at once a discovery of who God is and a discovery of what our mission as human beings on earth is.

On the basis of his historical and hermeneutical investigations Schillebeeckx proposes that the distinctiveness, uniqueness, and foundation of Christianity "lies in Jesus' message and praxis of the kingdom of God, with all its consequences."[89] If this message and praxis of Jesus is to see its fruition in God's kingdom, then "the history of Jesus' career must be continued in his disciples." Without this continuity by the Christian community, the Church, Jesus's proclamation and praxis will remain in "a purely speculative, empty vacuum."[90] "Christ" will be no more than an honorific title if the redemption began in Jesus is not continued but ends with his death and resurrection. "It is not the confession 'Jesus is Lord' (Rom 10:9) which in itself brings redemption, but 'he who does the will of my Father' (Matt 7:21)."[91] If God's offer of salvation in Jesus is to be truly universal—meaning, that it is valid and open to all—then the church has to be active in continuing Jesus's mission by following his way of life.

This means that Christians, the community of disciples, have to "take upon themselves the aspirations of the wronged of this world and [be] in solidarity with the call for justice of poor and voiceless people."[92] As justice and peace are the entitlements of all persons, and not only for Christians,

---

87. Schillebeeckx, *Jesus*, 601.
88. Ibid., 602.
89. Schillebeeckx, *Church*, 165.
90. Ibid., 168.
91. Ibid.
92. Ibid., 169.

the salvation in Jesus has to be universalized through Christian praxis. It is the mission of Christians, "called to be God's holy people," to "confess freedom from evil," to undertake "the task of bringing justice," and to be filled with "the courage to love." Schillebeeckx is emphatic that "the transformation of the world to a higher humanity, to justice and peace, is therefore an essential part of the 'catholicity' or universality of Christian faith; and this is *par excellence* a non-discriminatory universality."[93]

Schillebeeckx then adds that God—as revealed in Jesus of Nazareth—who is "the creator, the foundation, source and horizon of the eschatological or final unity of world history," cannot remain the "private possession of the Christian churches." Rather, God must be the object and subject of Christian mission, where mission is never "narrowed down to a form of collaboration in development" but a bearing witness to Jesus Christ as a means to furthering "God's kingdom of justice and love throughout the world."[94] Specifically, "as prophet, the missioner must go and stand alongside the oppressed in the struggle which in fact is being carried on for more humanity and salvation."[95] This is the witness to the gospel and this is the story that disciples of Jesus are asked to tell, in word as well as in deed. Bringing the gospel to the oppressed and the marginalized is effected "not only through words but through solidarity in action and thus through a praxis of liberation."[96]

Mission, therefore, "comprises evangelization and collaboration in development and the work of liberation: caritative and political diakonia."[97] In mission, the Church—not synonymous with the kingdom—is "given second place."[98] Having said that, it is still important for Christians to "create new groups which also themselves hand on the torch and, in the footsteps of Jesus, share in God's saving initiative." The notion of "conversion" remains an important priority in Christian mission, except that it is understood in a non-discriminatory fashion and given to mean conversion to God's kingdom rather than to the Roman Catholic Church. Hence, "the Christian message of the kingdom of God with its potential

93. Ibid., 170.
94. Ibid., 183.
95. Ibid., 184.
96. Ibid., 185.
97. Ibid., 184.
98. Ibid., 183.

for liberation remains in its distinctive character an offer to all men and women."[99] Individuals, as well as whole cultures and religions, can be evangelized and challenged to a more authentic conversion in view of furthering the kingdom of God. The Catholic Church also stands in need of such evangelization and challenge from other religions and persons of goodwill.

Such is the "new heaven" and the "new earth" that Schillebeeckx confesses in his creed, and such is his "hope for a life with God and with one another for all eternity." With St. Ireneaus, Schillebeeckx underscores in his "Jesus books" that salvation for all of humankind lies in the living God, the creator of all (*vita hominis, visio Dei*), as well as the conviction that God's glory lies in humankind's happiness, salvation, and wholeness (*Gloria Dei, vivens homo*): "Glory for God and peace for men."[100]

STORY, THEOLOGY, AND PRAXIS

Schillebeeckx's trilogy is unique in that it grounds itself in the three components of theological reflection, viz., story, theology, and praxis. This is in keeping with his own thesis that the theological task must not only consist of theory but that theories ought to be combined with stories and followed by praxis.[101] In the trilogy the telling of the story is accomplished in *Jesus*, the theologizing on the early Church's experience of salvation is done in *Christ*, and the reflection on what all these mean as a matter of Christian praxis is the concern of *Church*. Thus, *Jesus*, *Christ*, and *Church* are the three separate but integral components of Schillebeeckx's theological reflections.

Each component contributes to the understanding and validation of one another. Stories function as the potent and critical force that converts and heals—as depicted in Schillebeeckx's recounting of Bultmann's paralyzed man telling a story so captivating that he himself began to leap and dance[102] —while praxis witnesses to the credibility of the theology. Without these, theology risks being no more than a task that produces sterile and abstract theories or ideologies that have not the slightest bearing on the contemporary and real world.

---

99. Ibid., 185.
100. Schillebeeckx, *Interim*, 142–43.
101. Schillebeeckx, *Jesus*, 673.
102. Ibid., 674.

Story, theology, and praxis, therefore, are the unique but intertwined aspects for any theological task. Taking the three books of *Jesus*, *Christ*, and *Church* together gives us at once a synthesis of the whole of Schillebeeckx's theology as well as a peek into his inner life of faith. Schillebeeckx himself regards his works as "a Christian confession of faith of a consistently rational theologian, who is conscious of standing in the great Catholic tradition on the basis of which he may be able to, indeed has to, say something—*as an offer*—to his fellow men and women."[103] The trilogy, therefore, is as much a work of theology as it is a confession of faith. It is Schillebeeckx's way of proclaiming his Christian faith that "Jesus is Lord" (*Dominus Iesus*).

What we have seen from the preceding exploration is that Schillebeeckx's *Dominus Iesus* is certainly quite different in tone as in orientation from the Vatican's *Dominus Iesus*. While both are concerned with proclaiming the Lord Jesus, the thrust of their proclamations differs remarkably. A key to this difference is the theological method employed, as method determines product. The next chapter will explore this in greater detail.

---

103. Schillebeeckx, *Church*, xvi.

6

Towards Schillebeeckx's Theology of Dialogue

As pointed out in the last chapter, there is an obvious difference between the theology of the Vatican's declaration *Dominus Iesus* and that which we explored from Schillebeeckx's trilogy. Though both were developed within a Western context and addressing similar concerns, their outcomes differed quite radically. We noted that this was probably a function of theological methodology. Of significance is that the Vatican declaration employed a neo-scholastic method of doing theology while Schillebeeckx's was more contextual and correlational. One might remember the numerous times the Vatican document invokes the authority of the Church to posit the finality of particular Church teachings. The cognitive and intellectualist approach to faith pervasive in the document, as well as its apologetic stance, clearly reflect the neo-scholastic influence.

CHARACTERISTICS OF DOMINUS IESUS

American systematic theologian Charles Hefling delineates three characteristics distinctive of *Dominus Iesus*: (i) it is assertional, propositional, and dogmatic; it is what it says it is—a declaration; (ii) what it states it does not explain; and (iii) its statements are re-statements. It is a text composed mainly of quotations from Church teachings of the past.[1] *Dominus Iesus*, therefore, is notably neo-scholastic, taking as starting point statements or theses on Church teachings. To be sure, these teachings are clearly spelt out at the beginning of the document. It is worthwhile to reproduce them here, if for nothing else, to note the precision of the language used and the essence of the doctrines it seeks to defend:

---

1. Hefling, "Method and Meaning," 108.

the definitive and complete character of the revelation in Jesus Christ, the nature of Christian faith as compared with that of belief in other religions, the inspired nature of the books of Sacred Scripture, the personal unity between the Eternal Word and Jesus of Nazareth, the unity of the economy of the Incarnate Word and the Holy Spirit, the unicity and salvific universality of the mystery of Jesus Christ, the universal salvific mediation of the Church, the inseparability—while recognizing the distinction—of the kingdom of God, the kingdom of Christ, and the Church, and the subsistence of the one Church of Christ in one Catholic Church. (§4)

On the basis of these theses *Dominus Iesus* then goes about to verify them—in the neo-scholastic tradition—by appealing especially to the teaching authority of the Church. Hence the many times it instructs that something must be "firmly believed in," or that one must respond in "obedience of faith," or that one needs to offer "full submission of intellect and will." As if that wasn't enough it ends by appealing to papal authority: "Pope John Paul II, with sure knowledge and his apostolic authority, ratified and confirmed this declaration and ordered its publication." The entire document quotes lavishly from papal documents, aside from the other ecclesiastical documents such as the Second Vatican Council, Church Fathers, and Church teachings of old. Scripture is also cited, but primarily to verify the Church teachings. They serve as prooftexts, seemingly void of any contextual considerations. Biblical theologian Pheme Perkins suggests that "*Dominus Iesus* treats texts of scripture in the same way as warrants for dogmatic assertions that exist without context." This use (or misuse) of Biblical texts reduces them to the function of "evidence for a series of dogmatic hypotheses."[2] Another scripture scholar, Rui de Menezes of India, asks if "*Dominus Iesus* is really founded on the Gospels [or] whether the Scriptures are being misused such as would bail out the document."[3] Whatever it is, there is no doubt that the document faithfully adheres to the neo-scholastic method of doing theology. It seeks first to assert Church teachings—the immediate rule of faith—and then to verify the same through the various secondary sources—the remote rule of faith.

It has to be pointed out, however, that, seen in its proper context, neo-scholasticism was very much a theology that was responding to the challenges of its own time. "In the face of rationalist criticisms of revela-

---

2. Perkins, "New Testament Eschatology," 81.
3. Menezes, "Can Scripture?," 210.

tion and concrete forms of religion, neo-scholastic theology sought to develop an apologetic for revelation and for institutional religion. In the face of the rationalist advocacy of clear and distinct ideas, it sought to define as clearly as possible what constituted Christian revelation. . . . In a period of ecumenical controversy, it sought to delineate carefully—though defensively—the distinctiveness of Roman Catholic identity."[4] In short, neo-scholasticism was an appropriate theological response to the challenges of its time. It was very much a contextual theology in its own right, the context being the fideism of the post-Reformation world, the rationalism of modernity, as well as the general skepticism towards any efforts of ecumenism.

That *Dominus Iesus* employs the neo-scholastic method is another matter altogether. To use a historically and culturally conditioned theological method to address the issues of the twenty-first century is at best disingenuous. Indeed, the world has changed since the advent of neo-scholasticism, and Catholicism has transformed since the Second Vatican Council. *Dominus Iesus* could have employed other theological methods in its attempt to address the contextual realities of the day. Numerous methods have arisen precisely to respond to these contemporary realities and issues. They generally take as a starting point *Gaudium et Spes*' "signs of the times" teaching to postulate theological methods more responsive to each sign of the times. These are contextual methods of doing theology inasmuch as they arise from and are responses to a particular contextual experience.

But this does not seem to be the case with the Vatican declaration *Dominus Iesus*. It certainly does not take seriously the "signs of the times" method in postulating its theology. It employs a theological method that arose in a different context and under different circumstances to address the issues of religious pluralism. In so doing, the document smacks of anachronism. It is at best inconsistent with the contextual experience of the Church. Even if it did employ a more contextual method the document could not have been generalized to the rest of the world as if it was globally applicable. Each context is different and so deserves its own theological response. This calls into question *Dominus Iesus*' presumption that it is not only a "global theology," but that its theological response is the only one faithful to the Christian tradition.

---

4. Fiorenza, "Systematic Theology," 33–34.

CHARACTERISTICS OF SCHILLEBEECKX'S THEOLOGY

Turning now to Schillebeeckx, we remember that he too began his theological career in the neo-scholastic tradition. But contextual circumstances propelled him to make a methodological transition, turning to the hermeneutical-critical method in the 1960s. It was this latter method that was to exert a major influence on his christological tome and that set him apart as a Roman Catholic theologian, pioneering a field that was to develop in the global Church as contextual theologies in the decades to come.

The distinguishing elements of the hermeneutical-critical method can be discerned through what Schillebeeckx calls the "conjunctural" elements.[5] He speaks of historical change as occurring in three planes: (i) ephemeral changes are those that come and go; (ii) conjunctural changes are those that are more expansive, profound, and comprehensive with slower tempo and rate of change; and (iii) structural changes are those that occur over centuries and are hardly detectable. The conjunctural elements, therefore, serve as useful indices to the basic philosophical frameworks, recurring themes, and fundamental convictions that guide theology. We will now attempt a discernment of these to see how they give shape to the content of Schillebeeckx's own theological reflections. This can best be reviewed by looking at how Robert Schreiter, one of the world's leading Schillebeeckx scholars, captures these conjunctural elements through the following statement: "Schillebeeckx's work can be seen as the results of trying to *understand concrete, contemporary Christian experience.*"[6] Because every single word in this last phrase is loaded with meaning each will be expounded upon in view of capturing the essential thrust of Schillebeeckx's theology.

Understand

In his works of theology, Schillebeeckx's primary concern was to make sense of things. His was a quest for understanding; of what we believe, why we believe, and how we believe. Yes, it is the Anselmian *faith seeking understanding*. It is faith in God who is utterly gracious and good and who elicits trust and engenders relationship. That notwithstanding, it is also faith in God who is beyond all comprehension and understanding;

---

5. Schillebeeckx, *Jesus*, 577–79.
6. Schreiter, *Schillebeeckx Reader*, 10–19.

in short, God is ultimately a mystery. With such a faith Schillebeeckx endeavored in his theological investigations to lead others closer to this mystery of God. In this search, epistemology takes precedence over metaphysics or, rather, metaphysics and dogmatic assertions are but endpoints and not so much starting points in this search for knowledge and understanding about God.

His three "Jesus books," for example, attempt to understand how the early Christians confessed Jesus as Lord by investigating the Christian movement rather than by taking the metaphysical christological faith confessions of the fourth and fifth centuries as starting point. Schillebeeckx's is certainly a down-to-earth theology that begins "from below," as it were. Such a theology, he believes, is more relevant to the contemporary Christian. In fact, the expressed purpose of his books was that they reach the ordinary Christian or would-be believer so as to assist them in their understanding of the faith. His motive, obviously, was pastoral rather than academic.

In his investigations Schillebeeckx was at ease to employ a variety of philosophical frameworks and theological methods. His early Thomistic influence, especially of "Thomas's relative optimism about the knowability of God by humans,"[7] greatly shaped his theology. He allowed himself to be challenged by the new hermeneutics, with its stress on the historicity of being, resulting in his being open to new modes of knowledge and understanding. Critical theory's insistence that as one makes sense of the world and searches for meaning and truth one also needs to be aware of the existence of nonsense, non-meaning, and non-truth greatly stretched Schillebeeckx's understanding of the meaning of understanding. As a result, he did not confine his quest for knowledge to any one hermeneutical framework but, instead, took the different perspectives seriously and integrated them into his theology.

This openness to methodological pluralism and his inclination not to subscribe to only one single system—or, better still, his anti-systematic approach—enabled him to achieve understandings in a variety of ways. Such openness is inherently accompanied by a non-absolutist approach to matters of faith and truth. Schillebeeckx is of the view that there can never be a normative system universal for all time and for all cultures. This conviction is no more than a manifestation of his acceptance of the

---

7. Ibid., 20.

historicity of being and thus the cultural and historical conditioning of all systems, including theology and language. Schillebeeckx comfortably embraces this sense of tentativeness as evidenced by the fact that at the end of his two mammoth "Jesus books" he still describes them as but prolegomena. He believes that ours is always "a word before the last word, a search for the right 'legomenon' or word."[8] We are but pilgrims in this search and, more importantly, we search with an openness that at the end of it all we may never quite realize that search in all its fullness. "This prompts Schillebeeckx to note on several occasions, as he does at the end of *Jesus*, that all theology must end in silence before the mystery."[9]

Concrete

Influenced by the moderate realism of St. Thomas, Schillebeeckx's works reflect an emphasis on the concrete rather than the abstract. This is in keeping with the shift in human consciousness towards a "this-worldly" orientation, where "man was beginning to accept the full value and dignity of his being man within this world."[10] Because God's revelation is seen as occurring in and through the mediation of the concrete and visible in human history, theology begins with concrete real-life experiences. "Revelation does not drop out of the sky as a series of truth; it comes to us in experience in concrete, existential encounter."[11] In the same vein, Christianity is viewed not so much as a religion of abstract revelations but as one of personal encounters. It is an encounter between the human and God in a dialogue. While the God-human dialogue goes on indefinitely, God has revealed Godself most definitively in bodily form through the God-human encounter in the incarnation of Jesus. Schillebeeckx speaks of this as the "primordial sacrament,"[12] a concrete and visible form of the God-human encounter in history.

This accounts for why Schillebeeckx intended his "Jesus books" as a response to the concrete questions believers raise about their faith. They are a theological attempt to help ordinary Christians understand their faith in Christ, with the hope that the God-human encounter is facili-

---

8. Schillebeeckx, *Christ*, 25.
9. Schreiter, *Schillebeeckx Reader*, 15.
10. Schillebeeckx, "Secularization of God," 59.
11. Schreiter, *Schillebeeckx Reader*, 17.
12. Schillebeeckx, *Christ the Sacrament*, 13.

tated. Schillebeeckx's theology takes as starting point the concrete human experience. As if to accentuate the point, Schillebeeckx begins *Jesus* with the story of a crippled man, an account familiar to many, everywhere and in every time. He ends the same with yet another story, about a paralytic who began to dance, which again is a concrete experience easily understood by everyone everywhere. It is within the embrace of these two stories of concrete day-to-day events that theology is done. Theology begins and ends with concrete events and actions; principles and theories captured in between are but subordinate to these concrete events of experiences and encounters.

If concreteness is the starting point, it is also the end point of Schillebeeckx's theology. Because the turn to "this world" is similarly accompanied by the turn to "the future," Schillebeeckx's concern also turned to the future. This is significant as the authenticity of faith can only ultimately be verified as an eschatological event, for "although the object of faith has indeed been realized, in Christ, it has only been realized as our promise and our future." Christian faith has to be concerned about the future, which "cannot be interpreted theoretically." Instead, "it has to be brought about." "Action (orthopraxis) must therefore be an inner element of the principle of verification," and serves as a critical indicator of the authenticity or orthodoxy of the Christian faith.[13] Put simply, faith "must be done." From the perspective of eschatological hope, the *humanum*, the kingdom of God, the salvation proclaimed and promised in Christ, can only be actualized through concrete human actions. It is thus that orthopraxis is the means—or royal road—to orthodoxy, a theme central to Schillebeeckx's theology. Just as God's action in history is revealed through concrete experiences, the Christian's expression of faith is made manifest also through concrete actions. Schillebeeckx expounds unequivocally that God's will of salvation takes place in the concrete realities of history: *extra mundum nulla salus* ("no salvation outside the world").[14] "Few theologians have insisted as seriously as has Schillebeeckx upon how concretely God acts in history."[15]

---

13. Schillebeeckx, *Understanding of Faith*, 58–59.
14. Schillebeeckx, *Church*, 12.
15. Schreiter, *Schillebeeckx Reader*, 17.

Contemporary

Another element which Schillebeeckx's theology is very insistent upon is the notion of the present. Theology has to address the present and contemporary situation. Just as Schillebeeckx was responding to the issues of his day and culture (of secularism and humanism), any theological enterprise today has also to take as starting point the contemporary issues in the setting in which the theologian is theologizing from. Thus, the hermeneutical process is one that is a mutually critical correlation between tradition and contemporary experience. Contemporary experience represents the hermeneutical situation from which one interprets the Christian tradition. These are the two sources of theology. "On the one hand we have the whole tradition of the experience of the great Jewish-Christian movement, and on the other hand the contemporary, new human experiences of both Christians and non-Christians." The human and social sciences and even the natural sciences contribute significantly to understanding the contemporary human experience. This second source, the contemporary situation, represents "an intrinsic and determinative element for understanding God's revelation in the history of Israel and of Jesus, which Christians have experienced as salvation from God for men and women, the first source."[16]

Because the first source of tradition (the Bible and Church teachings and practices of yesteryears) arose out of different eras and contexts, with the concomitant rules of their language game, they cannot simply be "applied" literally to the contemporary situation. They have to be translated and reformulated. We can only understand the past from the perspective of our present cultural and historical context, with its concomitant rules of the language game. What is required then is a mutually critical correlation "in which we attune our belief and action within the world in which we live, here and now, to what is expressed in the biblical tradition." Schillebeeckx spells out what this process of correlation entails:

1. an analysis of our present world or even worlds of experience.
2. an analysis of the constant structures of the fundamental Christian experience about which the New Testament and the rest of the Christian tradition of experience speak.

---

16. Schillebeeckx, *Interim Report*, 3.

3. the critical correlation and on occasion the critical confrontation of these two "sources."[17]

The structural constants that guided the response of Christians in the past, in accordance with their own respective cultural and social contexts, become the norm by which Christians of the present make their response in faith, in the language and medium of the present context. A fusion of horizons takes place, the result of which gives rise to a new hermeneutical situation. "In the end we have here the convergence of two stories, the story of the gospel tradition of faith and the story of our personal and social life which in the best instances has itself as it were become 'gospel': a fifth or umpteenth gospel."[18]

Christian

This leads us then to the question of the continuity of this "fifth gospel" to the Christian tradition. Schillebeeckx has always been concerned that his is a theology that keeps within the bounds of orthodoxy of the Christian faith. After all, he is postulating a "Christian" theology and so it has to resonate with the faith of the Christian tradition. Specifically, it must mean that the theology he posits is one that promotes a faith that is structured by the very same elements that structured the New Testament experience as well as the faith of the Christian community through the ages. Schillebeeckx posits "four formative principles which as a result of the same basic experience intrinsically hold together the different explanations of the New Testament," and which continue to structure the faith experience of the Christian community at all times and in all places. He describes these principles as follows:

1. A basic *theological* and *anthropological* principle: the belief that God wills to be the salvation for human beings, and wills to realize this salvation through our history in the midst of meaninglessness and the search for meaning; thus the finding of salvation in God coincides with man's realization of himself: to find salvation in God is at the same time to come to terms with oneself.

2. *Christological* mediation: the belief that it is Jesus of Nazareth who discloses perfectly and definitively God's start-

---

17. Ibid., 51.
18. Schillebeeckx, *Church*, 34.

ing point, and therefore where man too must really be concerned.

3. The message and life-style of the *Church*: the belief that this story of God in Jesus has been handed on so that it concerns us too: we ourselves can and may follow Jesus and thus write our own chapter in the ongoing living story of Jesus.

4. *Eschatological* fulfillment: the belief that this story cannot come to fulfillment within the earthly order of our history and therefore looks for an eschatological dénouement, for which the boundaries of our history are too narrow; belief, therefore in "already now" and "not yet."[19]

Against the backdrop of these four structural principles Schillebeeckx then posits three basic criteria by which Christian orthodoxy can be discerned. The first is the criterion of proportional norm. By this one compares the various interpretations of the faith over the years of Christian history to discern elements that are constant for the Christian faith. "If the various structures that have arisen in the course of history are compared with each other and, in this comparison, the key words of the biblical proclamation are taken as a referential framework, we certainly become aware of 'structural rules' which—even if the structure has lost its efficacy in a different social context—still preserve their intelligibility as models for every new structurisation."[20] A second verification principle of orthodoxy is to examine if the theological interpretation evokes a "doing of the faith." By this Schillebeeckx refers to the action that must accompany the belief that the proclamation of the gospel is the promise that the kingdom of God will come. "In interpreting the past in the light of the present, then, it should not be forgotten that eschatological faith imposes on the present the task of transcending itself, not only theoretically, but also as a change to be realized."[21] A third verification principle is that of the acceptance by the Christian community. A particular interpretation, if not accepted and received by the Christian community, remains but an interpretation and therefore not necessarily part of the faith of the Christian community. "Acceptance by the community of faith, or seen from a different point of

---

19. Schillebeeckx, *Interim Report*, 51–52.
20. Schillebeeckx, *Understanding of Faith*, 61.
21. Ibid., 66.

view, the *sensus fidelium* or consciousness of faith of the community, thus form an essential part of the principle of verification of orthodoxy."[22]

Aside from the particularly Christian orientation, Schillebeeckx is also concerned about how being Christian is correlated to being human. This concern "lies at the heart of the church-world issue" since the Christian is torn between being of the Church and being of the world. The fundamental questions that this situation raises are: "How does a Christian respond to this situation? How can one be truly Christian and truly human in this situation, since the two cannot ultimately be in contradiction?" As a response, Schillebeeckx draws on his "positive valuation of creation and God's activity within the world" to conclude that there is indeed no dichotomy between Church and world or between faith and life.[23] The world is where God acts and so it is also where the faith is lived. Where human beings are fully living and fully alive, Christian living is fully manifest. In the words of Irenaeus, "The glory of God is a living man; the life of man is the vision of God" (*Gloria Dei, vivens homo. Vita autem hominis, visio Dei*).[24] The Church-world problem, which is but an extension of the Christian-human problem, can best be resolved thus: "In the man Jesus, man's question about himself and the human answer to this question are translated into a divine question put to man and the divine answer to this question: Jesus is the Son of God, expressed in terms of humanity. He *is* the question-answer correlation."[25]

Experience

The notion of experience, even if discussed earlier, deserves special elucidation here, not only because Schillebeeckx spent a considerable amount of time and space on the subject but also because it represents the starting point of his theology. He begins the second of his "Jesus books," *Christ*, with an entire chapter discussing experience. Schillebeeckx regards experience as the medium through which human beings explore and receive the message of God's revelation and salvation. "God's revelation follows

---

22. Ibid., 72.
23. Schreiter, *Schillebeeckx Reader*, 13.
24. Schillebeeckx, *Interim Report*, 62.
25. Ibid., 100.

the course of human experiences. . . . There is no revelation without experience."[26]

It is against this backdrop that Schillebeeckx speaks of Christianity as beginning with an experience: "it began with an experience."[27] Experience is the source and foundation of Schillebeeckx's theology. Not only that; it is also its hope and goal. In his Jesus research, Schillebeeckx began by digging into the experience of the early Christian movement. His aim was to discover what it was in the encounter that elicited the change, the hope, and the trust that was to be found in these early disciples. This, he did, in view of enabling present-day Christians to similarly experience that same salvation which comes from God through this man of history, Jesus of Nazareth. It was the experience of life and hope that Schillebeeckx wished would be imparted to the present-day Christian. "Christianity is not a message which has to be believed, but an experience of faith which becomes a message, and as an explicit message seeks to offer a new possibility of life-experience to others who hear it from within their own experience of life."[28]

If revelation occurs in human experience Schillebeeckx regards negative contrast experiences as having "a revelatory significance *par excellence*."[29] It is in the experience of meaninglessness, innocent suffering, victimization, and oppression that human beings see God's plan gone awry. The threatened *humanum* is clearly a revelation that the world is not in order. Notwithstanding the positive and powerful experience of love and meaning abundant in the world, reality has it that the world we live in remains fundamentally wrong; evil and suffering prevails. This negative experience is regarded as a contrast experience because it more often than not evokes the critical resistance expressed as a fundamental "no" to the negative situation. The positive element resulting from the negative contrast experience is the expression of "human indignation," which "discloses an openness to another situation which has the right to our affirmative 'yes.'"[30] Such experiences of meaninglessness and suffering are of revelatory significance to us. They reveal our helplessness and finite-

26. Ibid., 11.
27. Schreiter, *Schillebeeckx Reader*, 129.
28. Schillebeeckx, *Interim Report*, 50.
29. Ibid., 28.
30. Ibid., 5–6.

ness, as well as help us get in touch "with a reality which is independent of us." They also point to the hope that such experiences elicit; a hope that, if manifest in the praxis of liberation and reconciliation, can bring about a change for a better world. "That is also a rational basis for solidarity between all people and for common commitment to a better world with a human face."[31] This solidarity and partnership with others can come about only through a process of interaction and dialogue, which is the topic of the ensuing sections.

CHURCH AS SACRAMENT OF DIALOGUE

The preceding discussions have clearly delineated the different theological methods adopted by the Roman document *Dominus Iesus* and the Flemish theologian Edward Schillebeeckx. On account of the difference in methodological approach, the sentiments expressed in their respective theologies seem to be at variance substantially from one another, even if both hail from a somewhat similar cultural context in Europe, albeit in different eras. This seems to suggest that the theological method employed wields a more significant influence upon one's theology than does the cultural context. That accounts for why the theology of the declaration *Dominus Iesus* has been less warmly received by those affected by the phenomenon of religious pluralism as would be the theology of Schillebeeckx.

For example, *Dominus Iesus* has a seemingly domineering and authoritarian tone, while Schillebeeckx's theology tends to be more tentative and conditional. *Dominus Iesus* appears to reveal clear-cut, resolute, and rigid teachings, while Schillebeeckx's theology is more inclined to display a sense of openness, indulgence, and even ambiguity. *Dominus Iesus* seems to take a somewhat confrontational and apologetic stance towards other religions, while Schillebeeckx's is generally acquiescent, accommodating, and even accepting of plurality and difference. The number of negative reactions from persons of other religions to the *Dominus Iesus* document testifies to the fact it was not too well received or appreciated, whereas Schillebeeckx's theology, and especially the way he theologizes about the uniqueness and universality of the "Lord Jesus" (*Dominus Iesus*), seems more acceptable to persons of other religions. In this regard, the very reason why the document *Dominus Iesus* was issued, namely, to address

---

31. Ibid., 28, 6.

the phenomenon of religious pluralism in view of proposing appropriate directions for interreligious relations, seems more ably addressed by Schillebeeckx's theology.

The foundations that undergird their respective theological methods make for the difference. Significantly, *Dominus Iesus* understands revelation as primarily a "deposit of faith" waiting to be communicated to others. Its theology suggests the Church as having the monopoly over this deposit of faith and so understands evangelization as the conversion of persons who are not Christians. This is alluded to in *Dominus Iesus*, which laments that despite the centuries of missionary activity, at the close of the second millennium, "the mission is still far from complete" (§2). Such a theology seems to be espousing the "fulfillment model" of mission, where other religions are seen as awaiting their fulfillment through Christ and the Church. Interreligious dialogue is seen as no more than a strategy and instrument for this evangelizing mission. *Dominus Iesus* expresses this unequivocally: "Interreligious dialogue, therefore, as part of her evangelizing mission, is just one of the actions of the Church in her mission *ad gentes*" (§22). In case there is ambiguity about what this "evangelizing mission" refers to, the document explicitly spells it out as the duty of the Church to proclaim "the necessity of conversion to Jesus Christ and of adherence to the Church through Baptism and the other sacraments, in order to participate fully in communion with God, the Father, Son and Holy Spirit" (§22).

On the other hand, Schillebeeckx's theology, which understands revelation as God acting in history, sees the Church's task as the discernment of this Word of God. This discernment has to be accompanied by the praxis of faith, in anticipation of the kingdom of God, the salvation for all. Following from this understanding, the mission of the Church is to invite all persons to "actually realizing salvation and liberation for all, in freedom, through a praxis in accordance with the gospel, in the steps of Jesus."[32] Such a theology espouses what can be regarded as the "partnership" model of mission, where the other religions are looked upon as partners and collaborators in the mission towards bringing about God's kingdom. As partners, each has a contributing role. The Church's role is unique, but so are the roles of the other religions. Each has a different role just as each has a different aspect of the message of truth. That these

---

32. Schillebeeckx, *Church*, 176.

differences are real can be discerned by the variety of beliefs and practices of the many religions. But the differences need not be looked upon as if they contradict one another; rather, they can be viewed as complementary. The task of interreligious dialogue is to discern how different religions complement one another so that together they may all work towards actualizing God's kingdom. Dialogue is not only useful, but necessary. It is imperative, for it is only through the dialogue with the other religions that the Church can discover the fuller aspects of God's will for humankind. In dialogue, the Church "allows itself to be challenged by other religions and challenges them in return on the basis of its own message."[33]

Such an orientation is in keeping with Pope Paul VI's call in his 1964 encyclical *Ecclesiam Suam*, promulgated in the ambience of the Second Vatican Council, which urged the Church to be a Church of dialogue. Paul VI meant this call for dialogue to be the new way of being Church. Schillebeeckx suggests that this call is a result of a basic attitude change within the Church. It is an attitude change in response to an ever-changing world and it is leading the Church to embrace the world with a sense of openness it had never displayed ever before. The Church sees itself as having a new role in the world, viz., to promote dialogue not only within the Church but outside of it as well. The Church is a "sacrament of dialogue." Schillebeeckx believes the Church is well poised for this role as evidenced by "certain fundamental changes in emphasis in the Church's understanding of herself."[34] These new understandings were appropriately articulated in the documents of the Second Vatican Council, which provides the blueprint for the Church to become a Church of dialogue. Schillebeeckx summarizes them as follows:

1. The earlier tendency to identify the Church too readily with the kingdom of God has been abandoned [LG, 5] and the idea of the Church as the people of God that is still on the way is more strongly emphasized [LG, 8, 9, 14, 21; UR, 2, 6; DV, 7; AA, 4; GS, 1, 40, 45; AG, 2].

2. The erroneous or crude interpretation given in the past to the idea of "outside the Church no salvation" has been superseded [AG, 7; GS, 22, 57; LG, 8, 16; NA, 1]. It is thus becoming increasingly clear that salvation is not the exclusive possession of the Church.

33. Schillebeeckx, "Religious and Human Ecumene," 256–57.
34. Schillebeeckx, "Church as Sacrament of Dialogue," 120.

3. The Roman Catholic Church recognizes the ecclesial character of non-Catholic Christian communities [*UR*, 3, 19; *LG*, 15; *GS*, 40; *AG*, 15].

4. She also recognizes the authentically religious aspects of non-Christian religions [*NA*, 2, 4; *LG*, 16] and even the presence of the Christian "new man," and therefore of Christianity itself, in all men of good will [*GS*, 22].

5. God's saving will is also more clearly recognized outside Israel and Christianity [*DV*, 3, 4; *LG*, 2, 16; *AG*, 7; *NA*, 1], with the result that it cannot strictly be denied that there are elements of revelation outside Israel and Christianity.

6. Emphasis is laid on the Church as the people of God before any distinction is made among the various offices in the Church, and specifically before the distinction is made between clergy and laity [*LG*, chap. 2 vs. chap. 3]. It is the whole Church as people of God which has received the anointing of the Spirit and, in its general priesthood [*LG*, 9, 10, 26, 34; *AA*, 3; *SC*, 14; *PO*, 2; *AG*, 15], is itself the active bearer of the unique Good News and of Christian tradition [*DV*, 8, 10].

7. Finally, the Council has affirmed the saving presence of God in the secular, political, social and economic evolution of mankind [*GS*, 26].[35]

With the mandate from the Second Vatican Council, the Church's task now is to discover its appropriate role as a "sacrament of dialogue." In the context of the issues raised by the document *Dominus Iesus* this search is even more urgent and critical. Of significance is that the Church has to discover its mission as facilitator of dialogue in a religiously pluralistic world. As it engages in this mission of dialogue the Church will be confronted to renew some of its previously held views and perceptions of the world and of the other religions. The Church will have no choice but to renew itself, its own self-understandings, and especially its theologies of other religions. Such is the task of the post-Vatican II Church if it wishes to take seriously the challenge of *ecclesia semper purificanda* ("the Church must constantly purify itself"): the Church has to be put in its place, as

---

35. Ibid., 120–22. The Council documents are abbreviated as follows: *LG* = *Lumen Gentium*; *UR* = *Unitatis Redintegratio*; *DV* = *Dei Verbum*; *AA* = *Apostolicum Actuositatem*; *GS* = *Gaudium et Spes*; *AG* = *Ad Gentes*; *NA* = *Nostra Aetate*; *SC* = *Sacrosanctum Concilium*; *PO* = *Presbyteratus Ordinis*.

well as given the place it is due.³⁶ In this regard, Georg Evers, a German theologian of Missio-Aachen who spent more than thirty years studying Asian theology, has this to suggest: it is the task of the Asian Church to take the lead since Asia is privileged with a hermeneutical situation where the Church exists in the midst of the many living religions of the world. The next chapter will be dedicated to the exploration of this task. As will be noticed by the end of the chapter, a lot of the themes and methods employed by Asian theology resemble those that Schillebeeckx's theology emphasizes. The next chapter could thus be regarded as an "application" of the theology and method of Schillebeeckx in the Asian context.

---

36. Schillebeeckx, *Church*, xix.

7

Toward an Asian Theology of Dialogue

IF THE VATICAN DECLARATION *Dominus Iesus* does not find a resonance in Schillebeeckx's theology, it comes as no surprise that its gulf and dissonance from Asian theology is even wider. Significantly, the declaration's neo-scholastic approach, with its reliance upon Greek and especially Aristotelian logic, has resulted in its overemphasis on the human function of reason (*ratio*). Revelation is spoken of in terms of a "body of truth" or the "deposit of faith," while religious faith is evidenced when one "assents" to this truth. Incidentally, a word search on the document *Dominus Iesus* reveals that the lexical item "truth" is used a total of fifty-seven times.

By contrast, the word "love" is used only six times and the word "justice" a grand total of zero times! Indian theologian Francis D'Sa points out that this is one of the major "heresies" of the document. He reminds that religious faith can only be "known from its effects: love, joy, peace, patience, kindness, goodness, faithfulness, gentleness, and self-control (Gal 5:22)," and not by one's knowledge of the "truth."[1] If in *Dominus Iesus* the accent is on logical reason and truth, in Asia one could say that the accent is on the elements of praxis, viz., love, peace, justice, etc. Again, if in *Dominus Iesus* the emphasis is on the cognitive experience of the mind, in Asia it is on the affective experience of the heart and of the will.

As can be seen from above, the theological thrusts of Asian theologies are the very same ones that Schillebeeckx's theology and method emphasize. For him, as for Asian theologians, theology has to take seriously the context and one's experience, the fruits of which are expressed in loving action and not dogmatic statements. Thus, Schillebeeckx's

---

1. D'Sa, "*Dominus Jesus*," 200.

hermeneutical-critical method of doing theology can certainly help in the understanding of and appreciation for Asian theologies. In fact, many Asian theologians have been employing elements of the same theological method, especially in negotiating the phenomenon of religious pluralism. This, as was elucidated in chapter 1, is but part of the global ongoing renewal on account of the Second Vatican Council.

RELIGIOUS PLURALISM AS AN ASIAN PROBLEM

The problem that gave rise to the Vatican declaration *Dominus Iesus* was religious pluralism. This, as noted in chapter 2, is in a way an "Asian problem." It is simply not possible for the neo-scholastic method to be employed to address the issues to which religious pluralism give rise to without taking into consideration the ground realities of Christians living in Asia. Georg Evers puts it rather bluntly: in light of the "new questions and problems posed by the phenomenon of religious pluralism," it is disingenuous that we "turn to the stock of old answers and traditional theological method and declare that the new answers are lacking and not compatible with the Catholic faith." What is needed, instead, is for the issues the Congregation for the Doctrine of the Faith is concerned about to be noted. They are legitimate concerns. Then, because this is an "Asian problem," "the Asian Churches and theologians [ought to be] called to be the pioneers to do the original theological work from their particular experiences, in order to help the wider theological community to find new orientation and agreement."[2]

Evers takes the case further by pointing out that "there are certainly important differences in the ways of thinking, perceiving, and expressing ideas between the West and the East." For example, it is not easy to simply translate Western dogmatic concepts, "which originated in the Greek-Latin philosophical and linguistic traditions, into Asian languages with their so vastly different language games, cultural and religious, as well as philosophical traditions."[3] Furthermore, *Dominus Iesus*' preoccupation with issues of singularity, oneness, unicity, uniqueness, and universality does not necessarily resonate with the concerns of Eastern culture, which lays little emphasis on a unitary system or worldview based on conceptual identities. Indian theologian Jacob Parappally suggests that "for those

2. Evers, "Recognise Creativity of Churches," 189, 192.
3. Ibid., 190.

whose world-view operates on the epistemological principle of identity rather than on the principle of contradiction" such exclusivity seems out of place.[4] Instead, plurality and ambiguity are appreciated more, especially in matters as ambivalent as faith and religion.

Another Indian theologian, Felix Wilfred, elaborates on this by suggesting that while the Western worldview is architectonic, the Asian is organic. The architectonic worldview, based upon a reality conceived in terms of individuality and separateness, is emphatic about distributive justice "because there needs to be some kind of balancing among the parts." The organic worldview, on the other hand, with a reality conceived in terms of relationship among the parts, is emphatic about the harmonious integration of the community, where harmony is defined as "the quality of *being* of reality in its plurality and unity."[5]

It makes sense, therefore, for Asian Christians to give due diligence to the value of relationship when theologizing about other religions. In this regard it is easy to understand why the Federation of Asian Bishops' Conferences (FABC) advocated that theology should be done through the mode of "dialogue." By this is meant that Asian theology is done through the process of dialogue. This, as will be seen below, is the new way of doing theology. Asian theology has to be dialogical in form as in essence. It is a theology of dialogue.

THEOLOGY OF DIALOGUE: THEORY

An examination of FABC documents, products of the post-Vatican II spirit of openness to the world, reveals that the concept of dialogue features prominently in the Asian Church's theology. In its very first meeting in 1970, called the *Asian Bishops' Meeting*, the Asian bishops had this to say: "In the spirit of collegiality and dialogue so earnestly urged on us by the decrees of the Second Vatican Council, . . . we have sought to discover new ways through which we may be of greater and more effective service—not to our Catholic communities only—but to our own peoples and to the future, pregnant with both fear and promise, which opens up before us" (*ABM*, §2). At the end of the meeting, through the resolutions, the Asian bishops pledged themselves "to an open, sincere, and continuing dialogue with our brothers of other great religions of Asia, that we

---

4. Parappally, "Profession and Proclamation," 226.
5. Wilfred, "Theology Harmony," 147–51.

may learn from one another how to enrich ourselves spiritually and how to work more effectively together on our common task of total human development" (*ABM*, §12).[6] Throughout the thirty years of FABC's existence this theme of dialogue kept emerging at practically every assembly and seminar, prompting Felix Wilfred to assert that the word "dialogue" can more or less summarize the entire orientation of the FABC.[7] Dialogue is the way of being Church in Asia. Dialogue is also the method of doing theology in Asia. In short, dialogue is the life and mode of the Asian Church.

Lest it be construed that the Asian Church's commitment to dialogue arose only as a response to the spirit of Vatican II, it has to be pointed out that it was also as much a response to Asia's own contextual realities. Specifically, its history and sociocultural context have urged the Church to inculturate itself and develop a more contextualized approach in its theology. As shall be seen later in this chapter, this contextual approach takes as starting point the realities and experiences of the Asian Church, some of which are discussed below.

Colonial Roots of the Church in Asia

One point which is often made about the Church in Asia is its foreignness. The Seventh Plenary Assembly of the FABC, held in the year 2000, emphasized the need for the "Asianness" of the Church to emerge.[8] This might sound strange given that the Church has been in Asia for more than half a millennium. Suffice to say here that it is in view of its history that the issue of foreignness has been a major stigma on Christianity in Asia in general. An earlier FABC theological consultation on evangelization in Asia outlined the issues pointedly:

> As a social institution the Church is perceived as a foreign body in its colonial origins while other world religions are not. The lingering image survives in its traditional ecclesiastical structures and economic dependence on the West. This gives ground for suspicion. The Church is even sometimes seen as an obstacle or threat to national integration and to religious and cultural identity. Alignments between the Church and socio-political elites often legitimize and preserve the socio-political *status quo* and do not

---

6. Rosales and Arevalo, *Peoples of Asia*, 1:3, 9.
7. Wilfred, "Orientations, Challenges," xxiii.
8. Eilers, *All Peoples of Asia*, 3:8.

succeed in obviating this image. The Church remains foreign in its lifestyle, in its institutional structure, in its worship, and in its western-trained leadership and in its theology. (§13)[9]

It makes sense, therefore, that the priority for the Church in Asia is to develop an appropriate local Church with a truly Asian identity. An ideological critique of the past, the old model of being Church in Asia, is necessary in order to discern why there exists the enmity and hostility towards the Church. The most relevant datum on this is that generally the Church of Christ came to Asia along with the European colonial expansion. It is therefore inevitable that the Church is associated with the imperial powers. It is thus a fact of history that the cross of Christ came together with swords and guns as well as the looting barrels, in what Aloysius Pieris calls the "unholy alliance of the missionary, the military and the merchant."[10] Just as the imperialists' aim was the plunder of the resources of Asia, the Church was also viewed as coming to plunder the souls of the people of Asia. This perception was not without its basis, as Christian missionaries "often adopted the attitude that non-Christian religions were simply the work of Satan and the missionaries' task was to convert from error to knowledge of the truth."[11]

It is not surprising then that the early missionaries had little respect for the people of Asia, much less their cultures and religions. The late Indian theologian Stanley Samartha illustrates this situation appropriately by drawing an analogy with the arrival of a helicopter in Asia.[12] When descending upon Asia—from above, of course—the helicopter blew away all that was on the ground to pave the way for the European Church to land. It also made so much missiological noise that the people of Asia were so annoyed that they not only rejected its message but regarded whatever the Church had to offer with hostility and suspicion. The Church, on its part, made little effort at adapting its message to the culture of the people; instead, it practically transplanted the norms and patterns of the Church in Europe to the lands of Asia. Such a transplanted Church never took root in Asian soil and so remained largely a European Church, even after having been in Asia for several centuries.

9. Rosales and Arevalo, *All Peoples of Asia*, 1:337.
10. Pieris, "Asia's Non-Semitic Religions," 50.
11. Abbott, *Documents of Vatican II*, 662.
12. Samartha, *One Christ*, 115.

Inculturating the Church in Asia

What is needed of the Church in Asia is an authentic process of inculturation or contextualization, one that takes seriously the world of Asia, in particular the plurality of its cultures, the diversity of its religions, and the distress of its poor. Using Samartha again, one can describe the nature of this inculturation by depicting the Church as a bullock-cart. A vehicle indigenous to Asia, the bullock-cart portrays a Church that is at once truly native and local as well as modest and humble. Coming from below and in touch with Asian soil, the bullock-cart Church is certainly more in touch with the people, religions, and cultures of Asia. It is therefore a Church that is more acceptable to the people of Asia. Just as it is necessary for the bullock-cart to be in continuous contact and friction with the ground for it to move forward, the Church too must be in continuous contact and friction with the people and religions of Asia if it wants to move forward. Contact and friction are therefore the modes by which the evangelizing mission of the bullock-cart Church is actualized.

Contextualization for the bullock-cart Church then refers to a mutually critical correlation and confrontation between Christianity and the other religions and cultures of Asia. This critical correlation and confrontation imply the process of dialogue. Dialogue, therefore, is the process by which the Church makes contact with the contextual realities of Asia. This process is as much for the purpose of enabling the Church to become more authentically local as it is for the purpose of enabling the people of other religions to better acquaint themselves with the Church. Through this process of dialogue the Church could hopefully become more acceptable to the people of Asia and be even regarded as one of Asia's own. It is in this context that the Church can be regarded as a facilitator or "sacrament of dialogue."

What are the elements of this dialogue? Who does the Church dialogue with and why should the Church do so? How does dialogue relate to the making of an Asian theology and what are the constituents of this theology? What are the peculiar characteristics that make for a distinctive theology in Asia and what does a theology of dialogue look like? These are questions to keep in mind as one attempts to postulate an Asian theology of dialogue. To begin the search, reference is made here to the wisdom of Aloysius Pieris, one of Asia's foremost contextual theologians. In his seminal article "Toward an Asian Theology of Liberation," Pieris writes:

Any discussion about Asian theology has to move between two poles: the *Third Worldness* of our continent and its peculiarly *Asian* character. More realistically and precisely, the common denominator linking Asia with the rest of the Third World is its overwhelming poverty. The specific character defining Asia within the other poor countries is its multifaceted religiousness. These two inseparable realities constitute in their interpenetration what might be designated as the *Asian context*, the matrix of any theology truly Asian.[13]

Evangelization through the Triple Dialogue

Contextual realities have influenced the Asian bishops so much that they have come to speak of the evangelizing mission of the Church as addressing the issues of poverty and attending to the religions of Asia. Such a mission is the task of the local Church. Hence, the priority is the creation of a local Church, a task that can be accomplished only through an integral process of what has come to be known in FABC documents as the "triple dialogue." Construing this as the threefold dialogue of the Church with the cultures, the religions, and the poor of Asia, the Asian bishops state categorically that this dialogue represents the primary means by which the Church evangelizes in Asia.

Advocating the triple dialogue, Pieris points out that the process of inculturation can never be effected by a mere translation or adaptation of Christian symbol systems. Inculturation, Pieris contends, "happens naturally." "It can never be induced artificially. The Christian tends to appropriate the symbols and mores of the human grouping around it only to the degree that it [the Church] immerses itself in their lives and struggles. That is to say, inculturation is the by-product of an *involvement* with a people rather than the conscious target of a program of action."[14] In the context of Asia, inculturation is brought about, first of all, through dialogue with Asia's poor, in view of facilitating their integral liberation. Secondly, because other religions have their own views of what liberation and salvation mean and because the majority of Asia's poor owe their allegiance to these other religions, the process of inculturation must also include the dialogue with the religions. In short, inculturation, interreligious dialogue, and the process of integral liberation are mutually involv-

---

13. Pieris, "Toward an Asian Theology," 69.
14. Pieris, "Asia's Non-Semitic Religions," 38.

ing ministries, all of which are integral to the evangelizing mission of the Church in Asia.

That Asia is poor is beyond dispute. It is therefore in need of the liberation that Jesus Christ offers and the Church can bring. It is precisely in this situation of massive poverty that the Church's mission of love and service is sorely needed. In other words, Jesus and the Church are necessary in Asia not so much because the majority of Asians are not Christians but because they are suffering and poor. Thus, any Asian contextual theology will have to take the fact of poverty, oppression, and exploitation seriously. More so if it is a Christian theology, since historically it was the Christian European West that committed a lot of the injustice of conquest, plunder, and domination upon the non-Christian Asian people of the East. By association, the Church has as much a responsibility as former colonial powers to alleviate the suffering of the poor in Asia and to address the root causes of injustice and oppression. Such a responsibility calls for a theology that has a liberative thrust to it, i.e., a theology that includes the element of praxis, leading to the reality of liberation.

Dialogue with Asia's Poor

This brings us to the question of how dialogue with other religions is related to dialogue with the poor. How do we integrate interreligious dialogue with the ministry on behalf of integral liberation? How do we get the people of other faiths to participate with us in the struggle against *mammon*? How is the Church accepted by the people of other faiths in the first place?

In addressing these questions, Pieris draws our attention to the works of Schillebeeckx, especially the part where he points to the idea that Jesus's baptism under John the Baptist was Jesus's first prophetic gesture.[15] Through this prophetic act, Pieris discerns four missiological principles relevant for the Church in Asia. Firstly, John the Baptist was from the Deuteronomic tradition of prophetic asceticism—one of liberative religiousness. Jesus opted for this brand of spirituality from among the many available during his time—the Zealots, the Essenes, the Pharisees, etc. Secondly, at the Jordan Jesus came before the Baptizer as well as those who had come to be baptized. The latter were the *anawim*, the poor, the outcast, the lepers, etc. By opting to be baptized instead of to baptize,

---

15. Ibid., 45–48.

Jesus joined the ranks of the latter group, identifying himself with the poor. Thirdly, by submitting himself to baptism Jesus received his missionary credentials. It was in his baptism, an event carried out in the presence of the poor, that he received his authority: "Hear ye him." Fourthly, the Jordan was a self-effacing act on Jesus's part. By submitting himself humbly to be baptized he was losing his identity. But, it was precisely in this loss of identity that Jesus discovers his authentic selfhood: the Lamb of God, God's beloved Son, the Messiah.

With his identity clarified and authority bestowed Jesus set off on his prophetic mission, a journey that saw him in defense of the poor and in confrontation with *mammon*. Pieris speaks of Jesus as God's defense pact with the poor and in a collision course with *mammon*.[16] It was this, especially his challenge of the ruling religious elites and colonial powers, that led to Jesus's death. The journey that began at Jordan in humility was to end on Calvary, not only in humility but also in shame; both the events, incidentally, have been described in the New Testament by the same word, "baptism" (Matt 3:13–15; Mark 10:35–40; Luke 12:50). "The baptism of the cross, therefore, is not only the price he paid for preaching the good news, but the basis of *all Christian discipleship* (Mark 8:34)."[17]

From Church in Asia to Church of Asia

The foregoing reflections clearly show that the task of developing a local Church has to be through the process of dialogue, where the term "dialogue" is used loosely to refer to the interactions, relationships, and involvement between one group and another. The dialogue with the contextual realities of Asia, therefore, demands that the Church takes seriously the people who make up the cultures and religions of Asia. In particular, the Church, as disciples of Jesus, must also walk in the footsteps of he who humbled himself in order to serve the poor of his time. The events that took place at Jordan and Calvary are significant markers that the Church in Asia can learn from.

Significantly, it was at the river Jordan that Jesus received his first baptism. This was a baptism into the religiousness of the culture of his time. It was through this act of baptism that Jesus received the necessary credentials to exercise his prophetic mission. Following in the footsteps

---

16. Pieris, *God's Reign*, 57.
17. Ibid., 49.

of Jesus, the Church in Asia has to also take this first step, which is to submit itself to a baptism by the river of Asia's religiousness. In effect this means that the Church must be extensively immersed and involved with Asia's other religions. Essentially this first step requires the Church to fulfill "the prophetic imperative to immerse [it]self in the baptismal waters of Asian religions" so that it becomes a local Church "'initiated' into the pre-Christian traditions under the tutelage of [Asia's] ancient gurus." Because this is something the Church has hitherto not done in many parts of Asia, it continues to lack the authority to minister to the people in Asia. In the words of Pieris, it would mean the Church "will continue to be an ecclesiastical complex full of 'power' but lacking in 'authority.'" In this baptism, the Church, like her Master Jesus, will have to simply "sit at the feet of Asian gurus not as an *ecclesia docens* (a teaching Church) but as an *ecclesia discens* (a learning Church), lost among the 'religious poor' of Asia, among the *anawim* who go to their gurus in search of the kingdom of holiness, justice, and peace."[18]

The second baptism that Jesus received, the one of Calvary, is even more significant. In current ecclesial language one could refer to it as the sacrament of confirmation. It was a confirmation of all of Jesus's signs, preaching, teachings, and actions, which began with the baptism of water at Jordan and ended with his execution in what Pieris calls "the baptism of the cross." This was "a cross that the money-polluted religiosity of his day planted on Calvary with the aid of a colonial power (Luke 23: 1–23)." It is not without connection that prior to arriving on Calvary Jesus's journey had taken him through terrains where he had openly challenged the status quo and ruling elites. His was a

> calculated strategy against *mammon* whom he declared to be God's rival (Matt 6:24). The kingdom he announced was certainly not for the rich (Luke 6: 20–26). It takes a miracle for a rich person to give up wealth and enter the kingdom (Mark 10: 26–27). His curses on the "haves" (Luke 6: 24–25) and his blessings on the "have-nots" (Luke 6: 20–23) are sharpened by his dictum that it is in and through the poor (the hungry, the naked, etc.) that he would pass his messianic judgment on entire nations (Matt 25: 31–46).[19]

---

18. Ibid., 47.
19. Ibid.

As the Asian bishops also realize, in the first *Bishops' Institute for Social Action* they had this to say: "opting to be with the poor involves risk of conflict with vested interests or 'establishments,' religious, economic, social, political. It also involves for leaders of the Church especially, *loss of security*, and that not only material but spiritual [as well]" (*BISA I*, §6).[20]

It is therefore quite clear that the only way by which the Church in Asia can discover its identity and acquire its authority is if it consciously submits to the challenge of other religions and the challenge of the poor. Unless the Asian Church is baptized in the "Jordan" of Asian religions and confirmed by the "Calvary" of Asian poverty, it will remain foreign and unacceptable by the majority of the people of Asia. Such is the process of inculturation and such is the challenge the Church knows it has to accept if it wants to become an authentically local Church in Asia. Realizing this, the Asian bishops, in their very first FABC plenary assembly, asserted that "the primary focus of our task of evangelization then, at this time in our history, is the building up of a truly local Church. . . . The local Church is a Church incarnate in a people, a Church indigenous and inculturated. And this means concretely a Church in continuous, humble and loving dialogue with the living traditions, the cultures, the religions"(*FABC I*, §9, 12).[21]

THEOLOGY OF DIALOGUE: METHOD

With the preceding discussion on the theoretical aspect of a theology of dialogue as backdrop, we turn now to look at how this is given form in the actual praxis of dialogue. As Schillebeeckx would emphasize, it is the "doing" that makes the dialogue come true. We will, therefore, look at what is entailed in the Asian Church's praxis of dialogue by focusing specifically on the dialogue with the religions, i.e., interreligious dialogue. These are the essential steps that need to be taken for the Church to move towards a Church of dialogue and for it to eventually become a sacrament of dialogue. The proposed paradigm employs the foundational elements of the praxis of dialogue taken by the Asian Church as revealed in FABC's programs and directives over the years. Just as the theory informs (or misinforms) the praxis, the praxis also refines (or corrupts) the theory.

---

20. Rosales and Arevalo, *All Peoples of Asia*, 1:200.
21. Ibid., 14.

This is the hermeneutical circle of the theory and praxis of interreligious dialogue.

Attitude Change: Formation for Dialogue

As pointed out by Schillebeeckx, the Second Vatican's openness to the world began with a basic attitude change within the Church in the period leading up to the 1960s. By the same token any dialogue with the religions or the poor also needs to begin with attitude change through a process of attitude formation. Thus, "formation for dialogue" should precede the actual praxis of dialogue. This is to enable fear, prejudices, misinformation, and apprehensions that Christians have towards persons of other religions to be addressed and corrected, if not altogether removed.

These formation programs could include the basic teachings and practices of the religions to be encountered so that potential advocates of dialogue might have at least some basic understandings of the religions of their dialogue partners. Otherwise, one might end up in situations where ignorance makes the dialogue experience not only embarrassing but also potentially dangerous. Another essential component that the formation program ought to include is the basic teachings of the Church with regard to interreligious dialogue. The late Indian archbishop Angelo Fernandes, one of the stalwarts who ushered forward the agenda of interreligious dialogue for the FABC, in advocating a thorough updating of theological education in Asian Churches, had this to say: "Among Christians themselves there are some with fundamentalist attitudes who refuse to accept the Church's new and positive understanding of non-Christian religions and their place in God's universal plan of salvation. . . . Other irrational fears are based on centuries of prejudice and/or ignorance of other religions. Someone has summed up the position in two words: arrogance and ignorance."[22]

Be with Them: Dialogue of Life

The second step in the praxis of dialogue is for Christians to have actual contact and interaction with people of other faiths. No amount of theory or theology can substitute for this concrete experience of the *other*. In most of Asia this could be regarded as a given, since Christians live amongst persons of other religions most of the time. It is thus that Asian

---

22. Fernandes, "Dialogue in Context," 554.

Christians have an environmental disposition towards interreligious dialogue since it is a common day-to-day occurrence.

Not only that, many Christians also have relatives and spouses who are believers of other religions. A number of bishops or priests in Indonesia or Thailand, for example, have family members who are Muslims or Buddhists; some even have parents who are *imams* or *bhikkus* or leaders of their Islamic or Buddhist religious communities respectively. Such concrete personal experiences "force" Christians to be committed to interreligious dialogue. This experience of ordinary day-to-day contact and interaction is what has been called the *dialogue of life*. It is an experience that most Asian Christians share, especially if they live as minorities in multireligious societies.

The *dialogue of life* refers to an active and committed relationship Christians have with their neighbors of other faiths. This includes witnessing to the values of the gospel, which could take a form as simple as teaching a child to love a friend of another faith or to respect the worship place of another religion. Or it could mean an act as mundane as visiting a person of another religion who is ill or assisting when s/he needs help. The Asian bishops are emphatic that this witness through the *dialogue of life* is integral to Christian living. It is part of Christian mission. In their fifth FABC plenary assembly they had this to say: "Mission includes being with the people, responding to their needs, with sensitiveness to the presence of God in cultures and other religious traditions, and witnessing to the values of God's Kingdom through presence, solidarity, sharing and word" (*FABC V*, §3.1.2).[23]

Collaborate with Them: Dialogue of Action

The next step, after the initial encounter and *dialogue of life*, would be to work together with persons of other religions. This is where Christians are exhorted to view persons of other religions not so much as competitors but as allies and partners in the Church's evangelizing mission. They are the Christian's collaborators and together with them the Christian confronts *mammon* in view of facilitating the *humanum*, the kingdom of God. This collaborative action is often referred to as the *dialogue of action*. In the words of the first Asian bishops' plenary assembly, it is a

---

23. Rosales and Arevalo, *All Peoples of Asia*, 1:280.

dialogue that "leads to a genuine commitment and effort to bring about social justice in our societies" (*FABC I*, §21).[24]

If a common platform or essence is needed for this *dialogue of action*, "the suffering of the masses can constitute that essence." "The experience of pain, the reality of injustice and oppression and human rights' transgressed ought to be the starting point as well as the guiding principle" for this category of dialogue.[25] The *dialogue of action* has as its principal aim the alleviation of the pain and suffering of humanity and also that of the earth. Felix Wilfred calls this "liberating dialogue," a blending together of the main concerns of interreligious dialogue and the ministry for integral liberation. It is a dialogue that insists that religions can and must play a central role in the liberation of the people and, more importantly, that they must do it together. It is a dialogue "centered on the victims," in view of the "common project of humanization" precisely because "religions have a great liberative potential."[26]

Acting together must begin with reflecting together. The Christian and her/his collaborators of other religions need to reflect together on what constitutes oppression, who are the suffering, why there is continued injustice, and what common values form the basis of the collaborative action. Michael Amaladoss insists that all of these cannot be defined on the basis of "some presumed natural law common to all or on some abstract rational philosophy considered universally valid." Instead, "they should evolve from an ongoing conversation between the different religious groups."[27] The conversations and reflections, in turn, must begin with experience. This means that a direct experience with the persons or community in pain is necessary, implying the need for the dialogue partners to be in direct contact with the suffering persons whose cause they intend to champion. The important point here is that they do it together—the Christian together with her/his collaborators of other religions. Thus, the *dialogue of action* presupposes the *dialogue of life* or "being with the *other*," where the *other* now refers to the poor, the suffering and the oppressed, as well as the partner of other religions. With time, these dialogue partners would have fostered such a relationship with the

24. Ibid., 15.
25. Chia, "Interreligious Dialogue," 124.
26. Wilfred, "Liberating Dialogue," 261–74.
27. Amaladoss, *Life in Freedom*, 202.

poor that they will not only be working for the poor but will be poor in spirit themselves.

Dialogue with Them: Dialogue of Discourse

It is only after having built relationships in the *dialogue of life* and having worked together in the *dialogue of action* that one should engage in the *dialogue of discourse*. This category of dialogue is variously called "dialogue of theology, "dialogue of creeds," or "dialogue of experts." As these names suggest this dialogue is the task of those who have specific knowledge of theology and especially comparative theology. It is a dialogue peculiar to trained scholars and happens most often in academic settings. It is the most published category of dialogue and for that reason is often mistakenly thought to be the only type of interreligious dialogue possible. That accounts for why those who perceive themselves as theologically incompetent feel they should not be involved in the ministry of dialogue.

The *dialogue of discourse* addresses all areas of religion, from comparing scripture to clarifying cultic practices to discussing doctrines and beliefs to analyzing the myths and stories of each other's religious tradition. It presumes that one engages in interfaith dialogue, as the philosopher of religion Wilhelm Dupre opines, not only because people from different faiths have different perspectives, "but in the understanding that their faiths are different too." Not only that, but "the awareness of [the] religious differences is indeed essential to inter-faith dialogue."[28] In acknowledging this the dialogues seek to discern and understand where different faiths are more likely to converge and/or diverge.

The dialogues are also important on three counts. Firstly, the very act of being in dialogue, which effectively means doing theology together with persons of other religions, significantly shapes the outcome of one's own theology. To be sure, theological statements that issue from such *dialogues of discourse* are not only extremely sensitive but also extremely positive of the *other*. Secondly, understanding another's religion through an actual process of dialogue is significantly different from the understanding one acquires from a process of book study. In the *dialogue of discourse* one learns about the other religion also through its embodiment in the life, speech, and actions of the dialogue partner. The whole being enters the negotiating table, and not merely the doctrines or teachings.

---

28. Dupre, "Implicit Religion," 29, 34.

Such dialogues are what Raimon Panikkar terms as "religious" or "sacred" events.[29] Thirdly, the *dialogue of discourse* is a dynamic process. It is constantly evolving. The more one learns about the *other*, the more one self-reflects and arrives at renewed understandings of one's own religion. This is self-critique that is engaged in as a response to the challenge posed by the encounter in dialogue. It is a response to the challenge upon one's pre-understandings on account of the new understandings gained through the process of dialogue. The fusion of horizons that takes place gives rise to a new hermeneusis, which in turn provides the new pre-understandings to apprehend a new hermeneutical situation. Through the new hermeneutical situation one then encounters the *other* again in a further *dialogue of discourse* and goes through the entire circle all over again. This cycle repeats itself resulting in a reflection process that is never-ending and impinges upon all other areas of faith and theological life.

Experience Religion with Them: Dialogue of Spirituality

The next step after the *dialogue of discourse* is for persons to have an opportunity to share in the religious experience of the dialogue partner. Also called "dialogue of spirituality" or "dialogue of religious experience" or "depth dialogue," this is the spiritual dimension of dialogue. How do we pray? Why do we pray? Who is God for us? What motivates us to live virtuously? These are some of the questions addressed in this category of dialogue. Our experiences in pilgrimages, a spiritual insight, a religious vision, or a prayer image are some of the contents of this dialogue.

As *dialogues of spirituality* entail the sharing of personal experiences which can at times be intimate, it is generally understood that there will be no arguments or discussions on what is shared. Instead, each dialogue partner is encouraged to share about the depths of her/his religious experience, with no concern for the rightness or wrongness of those experiences. This category of dialogue is by no means an occasion for debates or discussions and neither are they occasions for study or analysis. As religious experience, they remain personal and subjective and can only add to the treasury of how people experience their God and religion.

The *dialogue of spirituality* could also include periods of common worship or prayer where all the dialogue partners participate even if they are of different religions. The implications of this exercise are serious and

---

29. Panikkar, *Intrareligious Dialogue*, 69–70.

so have been addressed very cautiously by Rome, especially in light of its oversensitivity to doctrinal and practical syncretism and relativism. That accounts for why it created so much controversy when Pope John Paul II called for the day of prayer in Assisi. The pope had to specifically announce that the gathering was a coming "together to pray" and not "praying together." In his own words, "Praying together, that is, saying a common prayer, is out of the question, but it is possible to be present when others are praying.... This 'being together to pray' takes on a particularly deep and eloquent meaning insofar as all will be the ones next to the others to implore God for the gift that all humankind most needs today in order to survive: peace."[30]

CONJUNCTURAL ELEMENTS OF ASIAN THEOLOGY

Having looked at the theory and method of an Asian theology of dialogue, it is now time to discern the general principles that seem to be profound, expansive, and pervasive. We will delineate some of the main themes and basic presuppositions that Schillebeeckx would call the conjunctural elements for an Asian theology of dialogue.

Hermeneutics of Graduality

As is evident in the method outlined above, a theology of dialogue progresses slowly, patiently, and gradually. One has to take time to be appropriately prepared for the dialogue, be in contact with dialogue partners, work together on common projects, and then only should one engage in an actual *dialogue of discourse*. There are no shortcuts to this; dialogue is a tedious and enduring affair. Only if attended to steadfastly will it produce valuable and positive results. Along the same vein, the process of mission and evangelization has also to progress gradually. It can never be rushed. The Christian witnesses through love, service, and deeds in the *dialogue of life*. It is through simple acts of caring, sharing, and attending that others see Christ and come to accept the Church and Christianity. The tangible and practical must precede the abstract and metaphysical. The Christ of "rice and curry" speaks louder than the Christ who is *homoousios* with the Father. That accounts for why Mother Teresa was so well accepted in Asia. Hers was a mission of touch, of love, of service.

---

30. Pontifical Commission "Justitia et Pax," 236–37.

Likewise, a theology of dialogue must also begin with the concrete and practical. It has to start with the concrete act of being in dialogue and relationship with persons of other religions. Only after experiences such as the *dialogue of life* and the *dialogue of action* can the theologian attempt to engage in the *dialogue of discourse* and the *dialogue of spirituality*. More importantly, the latter two forms of dialogue have to be done together and with the dialogue partner and not merely in one's study room or chapel, independent of persons associated with the religion. It is only after this long and gradual immersion into the religious world of the *other* that one can then attempt to postulate a theology to understand the religion of the *other*. In other words, a theology of dialogue must be done gradually, and the theology that emerges from it must be regarded as at best a gradual understanding of the Mystery of Truth.

Hermeneutical Spiral

Following from the preceding principle, a theology of dialogue has to also take a hermeneutically spiral route. The more one discovers about the *other* the more one should return to the dialogue process in order to discover even more. The five steps delineated above in the method of a theology of dialogue are not meant to be linear, but circular and spiral. Upon attending to step A (**A**ttitude change), one moves on to step B (**B**e with them), after which one moves on to step C (**C**ollaborate with them) as well as return to step A concurrently. This return is for the purpose of renewing one's attitude towards the *other* after having been through the actual exposure experience of being with them at step B. Likewise, upon attending to step C, one moves on to step D (**D**ialogue of discourse) but at the same time returns to step A and step B in order to spend more time with the *other* in the daily *dialogue of life* or to refine one's attitude even further. Concurrently, one must also move on to step E (**E**xperience religion with them) and engage in the *dialogue of spirituality*. In other words, there needs to be a going back and forth spiraling through the various steps of the dialogue process.

The step sequence, while intended to move one along gradually, does not imply a one-way movement. It is a multidirectional, circular, and spiral movement. Each step also builds upon an earlier step such that when one is engaged in the *dialogue of action* whatever lessons learned from the *dialogue of life* also serve to enhance the collaborative venture of the *dialogue of action*. More importantly, the earlier steps also need to be refined and cultivated as one engages in the further steps. The dialogue process creates fresh and new conditions and dispositions every step of the way and at every point in time, thus generating new hermeneutical situations for new dialogical encounters.

A theology of dialogue not only informs the praxis of dialogue; it is also the end result of or product of the praxis. It acts as starting as well as end point for the praxis of dialogue. Where the preposition "of" points to the nature or type of theology, it serves as starting point. In this case the theology *of* dialogue is an a priori theology that provides the necessary ideas and motivation to encourage the praxis of dialogue. Where the preposition "of" refers to the result of the dialogue, it marks the end point, the culmination of the praxis of dialogue. In this case the theology *of* dialogue is an a posteriori theology, a product of the dialogue activity or reflections attained after the fact and act of dialogue. In other words, as an a priori theology, the theology of dialogue serves to promote the praxis of dialogue. An outcome of this praxis of dialogue is gathered together in the a posteriori theology of dialogue. This latter theology then refines and renews the earlier theology and provides the basis for a new starting point to promote a new praxis of dialogue. The hermeneutical spiral repeats itself.

Hermeneutics of Praxis

As is obvious from the preceding discussion, the one single element that a theology of dialogue cannot do without is that of the actual praxis of dialogue. It is the "doing" of dialogue that makes the theology and it is also the "doing" that makes it unique. Dialogue is an active word, a word that necessitates some sort of action. Thus, a theology of dialogue can only come about precisely because there has been an act of dialogue. The praxis of dialogue is, therefore, critical to the formulation of a theology of dialogue. Without dialogue there will be no theology. Dialogue is the dynamic word—not theology.

Following liberation theology's assertion that the sociopolitical praxis of liberation is a hermeneutics for the discovery of truth, theologians of dialogue also assert that interreligious dialogue serves the same hermeneutics of praxis. It is a hermeneutics for the discovery of truth that is found as much in the world religions as in our own Christian religion.

Through the dialogue partner one learns about what is found in the *other*. More importantly, because of the dialogue partner one also learns more about what is found in one's own. This happens as dialogue provides the occasion for a self-critique of one's religion the way it would never be done if the *other* were not present. The presence of the *other* helps create an extra critical ambience through which we view the proclamation of our own faith. It is more than not wanting to offend the *other*; it is also about the extra sensitivity that arises on account of the *other*'s presence and that in turn gives rise to a broadened perspective. One consciously attempts to see things not only through one's own eyes but also through the eyes of the *other*. The praxis of dialogue, therefore, is in itself a disclosure event. It is as much a process of discernment as it is an event of revelation. God reveals Godself through the dialogical encounter, in and through the life and words of the dialogue partners, as well as in and through the dynamics and ambience of the dialogue process itself.

What are the implications of this praxis of dialogue? How is one to ensure that the process does not result in the loss of one's Christian identity? These are serious questions that need to be taken note of for those who seriously intend to pursue the path of dialogue. The guiding principles for authentic dialogue state that one needs to be, in the first place, grounded in one's own religion before participating in interreligious dialogue. The Christian is expected to be rooted in her/his own tradition or there can be no interreligious dialogue. At the same time this rootedness must be accompanied by a certain sense of openness where one is prepared to learn, to change, and to grow. Rootedness and relatedness, therefore, are the principal ingredients that guide interreligious dialogue. What is required of the committed Christian is the ability to "pass over" to the *other* in order to learn and to share, to give and to receive. It is, in the words of John Dunne, a "passing over from one culture to another, from one way of life to another, from one religion to another." Dunne's elaboration on this is apt: "The holy man of our time, it seems, is not a figure like Gotama or Jesus or Mohammed, a man who could found a world religion, but a figure like Gandhi, a man who passes over by sympathetic understanding from his own religion to other religions, and comes back again with new insight to his own. Passing over and coming back, it seems, is the spiritual adventure of our time."[31]

---

31. Dunne, *Way of Earth*, vii.

This, then, is the vocation of the Church in Asia: to be able to "pass over" and then "come back." It is another way of expressing the Asian Church's baptism in the Jordan of Asia's religiousness, made possible only through the authentic praxis of interreligious dialogue.

Hermeneutics of Pluralism

This brings the discussion to the issue of relativism, of which the document *Dominus Iesus* was written specifically to counter. Would such a "baptism" lead to the prospect of relativism? Does Christian faith not imply a sort of exclusivism since it entails claims to finality and to Christianity as the one true religion? These are pertinent questions and have been the subject of much theological debate since the rise of the hermeneutical method. They are precisely the stuff of interreligious theologies.

The FABC bishops were clearly cognizant of such questions. In a document entitled *Methodology of Asian Christian Theology*, the members of the Office of Theological Concerns ensured that these questions were addressed from the outset lest the discussion on Asian theology be grossly misunderstood. In fact, because the document addresses many of the same issues that *Dominus Iesus* raised, one could even say that the FABC document on theological methodology had anticipated the Vatican document or that it was a kind of response to the questions that issued from *Dominus Iesus*. The FABC bishops begin the document on the methodology of Asian Christian theology by distinguishing the notion of pluralism from relativism. Acknowledging that pluralism can easily slip into relativism, especially when not rooted, they end the discussion by saying: "just because certain persons and groups are misled in their search for truth, and just because they tend to perceive pluralism as relativism, or just because they tend to relativize all reality, we cannot conclude that all pluralism leads to relativism." Lest it is unclear as to what their own position is, the bishops then assert unequivocally: "reality is pluridimensional, and no one can deny the fact."[32]

In essence, FABC holds to the view that the notion of pluralism is somewhat more pronounced in Asian theology on account of the influence of "certain values that are paramount in Asian cultures arising from the various philosophical traditions and the concrete social-religious-cultural situations in which Asians live." Furthermore, the practical day-

---

32. Eilers, *All Peoples of Asia*, 3:334.

to-day experience of a sociopolitical climate "charged with communal tensions" in Asia has resulted in Asians being more concerned about the value of harmony amidst the sea of pluralism. "What is needed is a vision of unity and harmony, and a language of reconciled diversity that will enable people of different communities to work together for peace and the building of a more just society."[33] Such a vision facilitates the authentic acceptance of pluralism, including religious pluralism. As Michael Amaladoss puts it, "People then learn to relativize their own belief systems without in any way relativizing the Absolute to which they are committed and which they witness to and proclaim."[34]

ASIAN WAYS OF KNOWING

This Asian vision of unity and harmony is also often attributed to the different way in which Asians perceive reality, which in turn impinges upon their method of doing theology. A distinction is often drawn between the Western way of knowing and the Eastern or Asian way of knowing. This is expressed differently. Felix Wilfred's distinction between the "architectonic" Western worldview and the "organic" Asian worldviews is one way of expressing this.[35]

In summary, the former is often associated with the conceptual, rational, logical, analytical, mechanistic, and systematic, while the latter is associated with the experiential, symbolic, affective, intuitive, and holistic. The former stresses the distinction between being and hence betrays an immanent dualism (body/soul, subject/object, human/divine, secular/sacred, world/church, etc.), while the latter stressed interrelationship, complementarity, and a sense of psychic-cosmic interconnectedness. The architectonic worldview portrays identity as non-contradiction and so espouses a disjunctive *either/or* mindset, which has a tendency for exclusion, while the organic worldview's approach is one of identity-in-difference with the concomitant conjunctive *both/and* thought, which is wont to being inclusive. The architectonic worldview looks upon relationship with the divine as an interpersonal encounter, and so God is a personal being whom we encounter in an *I-Thou* relationship and whom we speak

---

33. Ibid., 330.

34. Amaladoss, "Church and Pluralism," 12.

35. Wilfred, "Toward Better Understanding." See also Painadath, "Interpersonal and Transpersonal."

to and receive in Word through revelation. On the other hand, the organic worldview perceives God as ineffable mystery whom we experience as the divine within the self in an *I-Self* relationship and whom we come before in the silence of our being in search of an experience of enlightenment. This latter view regards the God-human relationship as a transpersonal experience. The Western architectonic worldview conceives of religion as a body of truths, with an emphasis on doctrines, teachings, and beliefs, all of which are on the level of the intellect, the cognitive; the Eastern organic approach views religion as a way of life that has to do with right living, right conduct, and right practices, all of which are on the level of the affective and the will. For the former the aim of theology is to foster right thinking or orthodoxy, while for the latter it is to foster right living or orthopraxis.

Hence, when questions are raised about the unicity of Christ and of the Church or the priority of proclamation over dialogue or the necessity of salvation through the Church or the possibility of salvation of those who are not Christians, one can only conclude that they arose from the Western architectonic worldview. To Asian ears these questions seem strange, if not altogether irrelevant, because from an Asian organic worldview the distinctions, dichotomies, and exclusions are spurious rather than real. The Asian's answer to the questions would probably be: "Yes, Jesus is unique, but so are the other savior figures"; "Yes, the Church is necessary for salvation, but so are the other religions"; "Yes, proclamation has priority over dialogue, but so has dialogue over proclamation"; "Yes, the Bible is the inspired Word of God, but so are the other sacred scriptures."

This accounts for why the instinctive response from Asian Christians to the document *Dominus Iesus* was so dismissive. By the same token it also accounts for why the Vatican seems unduly worried about the direction Asian theologies are taking. There is the fear that this perceived spirit of relativism could relativize the message of Christ and of the Church. To be sure, the pluralism in theology engenders a lot of fear reactions. Suffice it to say that all of these are indications that the different worldviews matter just as do the different methods employed in doing theology. They are often at the root of East-West tensions, as made manifest in the tension between the Western Curia and the Asian Church.

However, it should also be clearly stated that Asian Christians are fully committed to their faith, just as they are very clear about their mission. With *Dominus Iesus* they believe that the Christian mission is the preaching of the gospel of Jesus, "the proclamation of the mystery of God, Father, Son and Holy Spirit, and the mystery of the incarnation of the Son, as saving event for all humanity" (§1). But, unlike *Dominus Iesus*, they do not necessarily agree on how this preaching is to be done.

Thus, as has been often repeated, the crux of the problem is not with the *who* of mission, but with the *how*. The answer to the *who* question, namely Jesus, is not in doubt. Asian Christians are in agreement that Jesus is the subject of their proclamation and, indeed, he has to be proclaimed. They, however, are not quite in agreement with the *how* question, namely the approach Christians ought to take in proclaiming Jesus. As the present study has shown, the Asian Christian's choice is through dialogue. Dialogue, for them, is simply the new way of being Church. It is the Christian's mission to be in dialogue. And it is in and through dialogue that the answer to the *how* question can be clarified. Thus, at the risk of belaboring the point, there is but only one way in which the Church can discern a response in the face of the challenge of religious pluralism: dialogue!

Conclusion

IN LIEU OF A CONCLUSION

IN KEEPING WITH THE thesis of the last chapter, a theology of dialogue is hermeneutically spiral in mode as in operation. That means the conclusion of the present study must remain tentative rather than definitive. Having postulated an Asian theology of dialogue, this must now be used to respond to new questions that arise as a result of the new perspectives formulated. The process repeats itself as the end of each cycle produces yet newer questions.

What the study has seen thus far is a paradigm for a contextual theology more adept at responding to the phenomenon of religious pluralism. This is an alternative to the Vatican declaration *Dominus Iesus*, which did not seem to have been too well received by the people of Asia. The document's theological method, which is of the neo-scholastic tradition, was deemed inadequate in addressing the contemporary challenges posed on Christian identity in religiously plural contexts. Another method had to be sought, and so Edward Schillebeeckx's hermeneutical-critical method was explored. Schillebeeckx, who was schooled in the neo-scholastic tradition, turned to this new theological method when confronted with the contextual realities of his time and culture. This method provides a basis for understanding the theology of dialogue advanced by the Asian Church. An Asian theology of dialogue appropriately addresses many of the issues raised by the Vatican declaration. Schillebeeckx's method, therefore, serves as a sort of bridge between *Dominus Iesus* and an Asian theology of dialogue.

The issues raised by *Dominus Iesus* are better addressed through the hermeneutical-critical theological method as it takes seriously the hermeneutical situation, which varies from context to context. The method is as valuable and effective for the Asian context as for Schillebeeckx's Dutch context. The important element in the hermeneutical-critical method is that the respective contextual experience is brought into a mutually critical correlation and confrontation with the Christian tradition. As each new hermeneutical situation raises new questions and requires new interpretations, to slavishly repeat an old doctrine and apply it to a new situation is being simply unfaithful to the Christian tradition. Putting new wine into old wineskins is at best disingenuous. This, by itself, raises the question of whether there can ever be a universal theology applicable to all. Is it at all possible for one single uniform formula of the faith to fit into every context and every era?

Following from the thesis of the hermeneutical spiral, the theology of dialogue that has been postulated is also subject to further questioning and reinterpretation. Having arrived at the end of the present study, more questions have probably arisen as have answers been given. For example, the research has to return to the initial question of whether an Asian theology of dialogue does indeed address the challenges posed by the phenomenon of religious pluralism. It has to address the question of the uniqueness and universality of Christ in relation to other religions and their savior figures. It has to address the question of the mission of the Church in multireligious contexts. While semblance of these critical issues have already been dealt with while postulating the theology of dialogue, it is in the actual praxis of dialogue that they can be confirmed and verified, if not challenged and modified. The praxis confirms or disproves the theory, just as the theory informs or misinforms the praxis. A theory without praxis, according to Schillebeeckx, remains an abstract ideology with no critical potent force.

It follows that the present study cannot make any form of definitive and conclusive claims. It has taken merely the first step, awaiting further steps. It has certainly not arrived at the last word. It remains a "prolegomenon," in search of the right and final "legomenon." It is therefore still at the experimental stages, much like Schillebeeckx's "Jesus books," which are but an experiment in Christology.

THE PRAXIS OF DIALOGUE

This means that the follow-up to the present study, namely, the actual praxis of interreligious dialogue, must be realized in actual dialogues if more specific conclusions are to be made. The necessary second step of actual face-to-face dialogue reinforces the thesis that theology must be "done." It cannot remain solely on the level of theory. The praxis of dialogue "makes" the theology of dialogue "come true."

That is why the last chapter was entitled "Toward an Asian Theology of Dialogue." It makes no pretensions about its limitations nor does it hide the fact that the praxis of dialogue is still in need of being more fully actualized. That is why the preposition "toward" is significant in the title. It points to the reality and shortcoming of the present situation and emphasizes the need to work toward realizing the fuller meaning of a theology of dialogue. It suggests that this theology has to be one aimed at promoting the praxis of interreligious dialogue. It does not suffice if it remains merely a theory.

This is where the Church in Asia remains essentially lacking: while a theology of dialogue has been developed, the praxis of dialogue is something that is still in need of greater development. What exists is a vision and blueprint for the contextualization of the Church in Asia rather than a history of interreligious encounters. Nevertheless, the FABC has been at the forefront of this vision, thus accounting for why the Asian Church is often viewed as progressive and prophetic by theologians from all over the world. The implementation of this vision, however, is another matter. It constitutes a serious problem and challenge for most of the local churches across Asia.

This problem is evidence of the deeper reality that despite efforts at inculturating and contextualizing the Christian faith, believers continue to resist the demands of these efforts. This is not surprising as, if we recall, the demands placed upon Christians who truly desire to live an inculturated faith are tremendous. Of significance is that one has to adopt a self-effacing attitude, which has no place for any triumphalistic display of the Christian faith. Such an attitude also embraces a kenotic spirituality, with the concomitant openness to learning from and with persons of other religions. These are great demands placed upon those whose Christian faith is, in the main, narrow and shallow. A truly mature faith, therefore, is an essential ingredient to developing a truly local Church that embraces the challenge posed by the theology of dialogue. This, unfortunately, is not a reality yet in the Asian Church. The theology of dialogue remains essentially a theory and a vision, and hitherto this vision has resided principally in the Asian Church's documents or theological journals.

But having the vision is itself already a significant accomplishment. Even if this vision has not been fully imbibed, its very existence is not an unimportant fact. At the very least it can be referred to as the preferred direction for the future of the Church in Asia. The praxis that is to follow the theory may take longer than desired. Nevertheless, without the theory the Asian Church would not even have a vision to guide it, nor a measure by which to evaluate its development. One therefore is thankful for an Asian theology of dialogue. It points towards the future promise of hope for a truly local Church that is at once authentically Asian and authentically Christian.

The same can also be said about the vision and directives of the Second Vatican Council. They too have yet to be fully implemented. Amidst counterforces within the Church actively working to impede its full implementation, the vision continues to unfold itself. The irruptions coming from the Church's periphery are on account of this vision of renewal. As this study has shown, the Asian Church's contribution to these irruptions is by no means insignificant. They are informed by the direction and vision that its own Asian theology of dialogue provides. With time, these irruptions from the periphery will affect the Church's center so much that the latter's yielding to the irruptions' demands is probably inevitable. *Dominus Iesus*, as indicated in the present study, is but a phase in the center's response to such irruptions. It is also an indication of the center's gradual yielding. While originally intended to arrest non-Roman ways of apprehending the phenomenon of religious pluralism, it might have indirectly achieved a completely reverse effect. Not only has it brought to the fore the critical issues surrounding the Church on account of the impact of religious pluralism, it has also evoked a response of "No! It can't be like this; we won't stand for it anymore" from the people of Asia. The Vatican declaration serves as a kind of "negative contrast experience" whereby the feeling of negativity towards the document is accompanied by a sense of positive hope for the future. This hope, expressed in critical opposition to what *Dominus Iesus* stipulates, has seen the Asian Church engaging seriously in reflection on what it means to be Church in Asia. A theology of dialogue that inspires such reflection insists that the Church be in continuous dialogue with all people, including those who represent the religions, cultures, and poor of Asia.

SOME TENTATIVE CONCLUSIONS

The preceding remarks, which return to the need for the praxis of dialogue, again point to the impossibility of postulating any sort of conclusion to the present study. Until and unless the praxis of dialogue is actualized, the theology of dialogue remains inconclusive, as it is but the theoretical component of a larger and integral theology entailing both the components of theory and praxis. But since the study has to be brought to a close, some features need to be discerned from the task of postulating an Asian theology of dialogue. For this purpose a quotation from a passage of Schillebeeckx's writings is employed to capture at least tentatively the essence of the theological enterprise:

> Theology cannot be simply a question of scholarship pursued within the walls of one's study, it can only be built up in dialogue with one's fellow-men, a dialogue which involves our whole lives, whether we shut ourselves off in anxiety or think together with others in hoping and seeking openness.... Even for the theologian himself, theology today is a personal, living struggle. He must try to solve a real, living problem which no one can wave aside by triumphantly—or is it desperately?—brandishing uninterpreted conciliar texts. He has to settle a genuine living question which has risen to the surface everywhere, and he must do this without succumbing to current slogans or allowing himself to be driven into a corner by pressure from those who follow the latest fashion and automatically dub him either an out-of-date conservative or a rash progressive. Faithful to the gospel and its vital presence in the Church and open to the real problem of living people, the theologian must, without respect of persons, be able to say with Newman: "I am going my way."[1]

From the passage above and by way of conclusion to the present study, with Schillebeeckx one discerns that theology is something to be "done" and that it is a tedious and exacting enterprise. It is done not by simply positing theological statements and doctrinal formulas that have no resonance with the lived reality of people. It is done not by a simple appeal to authority, be this the authority of Scripture and tradition or the pope and the Church's magisterium. It is done not by simply reflecting systematically and theologically, especially if these reflections are performed within the confines of one's study room. Theology is a flesh-and-

---

1. Schillebeeckx, "Epilogue," 170–71.

blood affair. It must involve the lives of people; it must take their human experience as starting point for theological reflections. The process is inductive, never deductive. It begins "from below," taking seriously the lived reality of people and the context of their world and culture. This is what it means to be engaged in the process of *dialogue*. Dialogue, therefore, refers to the systematic contacts, interactions, involvements, relationships, and conversations between the theologian and her/his surroundings.

This dialogue has no limits and entails all the interactions possible with what FABC has termed the "resources of theology" (*loci theologici*), which, the Asian bishops assert, must "assume methodological importance."[2] These resources include contextual realities such as "the cultures of peoples, the history of their struggles, their religions, their religious scriptures, oral traditions, popular religiosity, economic and political realities and world events, historical personages, stories of oppressed people crying for justice, freedom, dignity, life and solidarity." In short, the theologian has to be in dialogue with the whole of people's lives, their joys and hopes as well as their griefs and anxieties. It is through such dialogues that theology is done. The theologian's efforts and attitudes are by no means insignificant. Doing theology is not an easy task. As Schillebeeckx puts it, it is "personal" and is a "living struggle." Theology entails solving "a real, living problem" and not abstract reflections on issues with little bearing on people's existential lives. The theologian comes to the dialogue with little expectations and, to the extent that is possible, with no preconceived suppositions. The contextual realities speak and teach while the theologian listens and learns. God and Jesus Christ are discerned and discovered, rather than preached and proclaimed. The hermeneutical situation presents itself while the theologian brings her/his own pre-understandings to it to forge new understandings. Making sense of these new understandings, the theologian is discerning God's Word inasmuch as the fruits of the discernment promote new life.

Theology, therefore, is a life-giving enterprise and is always in the service of life. It has to move beyond the definition of "faith seeking understanding" to that of "faith seeking new life." It should not be merely a cerebral, intellectual, or cognitive activity dealing mainly with abstract issues of metaphysics and doctrinal concerns. Instead, it ought to be an affective and volitional enterprise dealing primarily with the concrete and

---

2. Eilers, *All Peoples of Asia*, 3:355–64.

practical issues of real life and its struggles. Theology ought to affect the whole of life and it is in that sense an integral and holistic endeavor. Its main purpose is pastoral and not academic. It ought to respond to the fundamental questions of Christian faith, such as: "Who do you say that I am?"; "What does salvation from God in Jesus mean?"; and "What is the Church's response to this offer of salvation?" But theology must do so in a practical and down-to-earth manner. Its answers should then be accessible to, understandable by, and applicable to the believing Christian in the concrete experience of daily life. It effects change and transformation in such a way the believer becomes more life-giving and more concerned about others and of the world. This is the faith response that results from theological reflection if such reflection includes both a critical intention and the element of praxis. Such a theology evokes the praxis of Christian living in a practical anticipation of God's kingdom here on earth. It is then that we proclaim *Dominus Iesus*!

Bibliography

Abbott, Walter, editor. *The Documents of Vatican II.* Piscataway, NJ: New Century, 1966.
Allen, John L. *Cardinal Ratzinger: The Vatican's Enforcer of the Faith.* New York: Continuum, 2000.
———. "De Mello Censure Reflects Vatican Misgivings about Eastern Thinking." *National Catholic Reporter,* 4 September 1998. Online: http://natcath.org/NCR_Online/archives2/1998c/090498/090498k.htm.
———. "Gap Between Theory, Reality." *National Catholic Reporter,* 22 September 2000. Online: http://natcath.org/NCR_Online/archives2/2000c/092200/092200f.htm.
Amaladoss, Michael. "The Church and Pluralism in the Asia of the 1990s." In *FABC Papers No. 57e,* 1–19. Hong Kong: FABC, 1990.
———. "'Do Not Judge . . .' (Matt 7:1)." *Jeevadhara* 31.183 (May 2001) 179–82.
———. *Life in Freedom: Liberation Theologies from Asia.* Anand: Gujarat Sahitya Prakash, 1997.
Balasuriya, Tissa. *Mary and Human Liberation: The Story and the Text.* Harrisburg, PA: Trinity, 1997.
———. "A Thank You and an Interim Reflection on the Reconciliation." *East Asian Pastoral Review* 35.2 (1998) 249–53.
"Bishops Note Room for 'Theological Inquiry' in Toning Down 'Dominus Iesus.'" *Union of Catholic Asian News,* 3 May 2001. Online: http://www.ucanews.com/story-archive/?post_name=/2001/05/03/bishops-note-room-for-theological-inquiry-in-toning-down-dominus-iesus&post_id=18353.
Bowden, John Stephen. *Edward Schillebeeckx: Portrait of a Theologian.* London: SCM, 1983.
"Cardinal Cassidy Appeals to Jews to Renew Dialogue: Promoter of Ecumenism Believes 'Dominus Iesus' Declaration Is Misunderstood." *ZENIT,* 26 September 2000. Online: http://www.alliancenet.org/partner/Article_Display_Page/0,,PTID5339_CHID28_CIID156511,00.html.
Chia, Edmund. "Interreligious Dialogue for Human Promotion and Human Rights." In *Human Promotion and Human Rights in the Third Millennium: Reconciliation and Solidarity, Our Options for the Third Millenium,* edited by Anthony Rogers, 121–30. Manila: FABC Office for Human Development, 1999.
Coleman, John Aloysius. *The Evolution of Dutch Catholicism, 1958–1974.* Berkeley: University of California, 1978.
Congregation for the Doctrine of the Faith. Declaration *Dominus Iesus* on the Unicity and Salvific Universality of Jesus Christ and the Church. August 6, 2000. Online: http://www.vatican.va/roman_curia/congregations/cfaith/documents/rc_con_cfaith_doc_20000806_dominus-iesus_en.html.

———. "Instruction on Certain Aspects of the 'Theology of Liberation'" (*Libertatis nuntius*). March 22, 1986. Online: http://www.vatican.va/roman_curia/congregations/cfaith/documents/rc_con_cfaith_doc_19860322_freedom-liberation_en.html.

———. "Instruction on Christian Freedom and Liberation" (*Libertatis conscientia*). March 22, 1986. Online: http://www.vatican.va/roman_curia/congregations/cfaith/documents/rc_con_cfaith_doc_19860322_freedom-liberation_en.html.

———. "Notification on the Book *Toward a Christian Theology of Religious Pluralism* by Fr. Jacques Dupuis, S.J." January 24, 2001. Online: http://www.vatican.va/roman_curia/congregations/cfaith/documents/rc_con_cfaith_doc_20010124_dupuis_en.html.

———. "Notification Concerning the Text 'Mary and Human Liberation' by Father Tissa Balasuriya, OMI." January 2, 1997. Online: http://www.vatican.va/roman_curia/congregations/cfaith/documents/rc_con_cfaith_doc_19970102_tissa-balasuriya_en.html.

———. "Notification: Concerning the Writings of Father Anthony De Mello, S.J." June 24, 1998. Online: http://www.vatican.va/roman_curia/congregations/cfaith/documents/rc_con_cfaith_doc_19980624_demello_en.html.

"'*Dominus Iesus*' Brings Cultural Tension for Vietnam Catholics." *Union of Catholic Asian News*, 18 September 2000. Online: http://www.ucanews.com/story-archive/?post_name=/2000/09/18/dominus-iesus-brings-cultural-tension-for-vietnam-catholics&post_id=541.

D'Sa, Francis. "*Dominus Jesus* and Modern Heresies." *Jeevadhara* 31.183 (May 2001) 197–202.

Dunne, John S. *The Way of All the Earth: An Encounter with Eastern Religions*. London: Sheldon, 1972.

Dupre, Wilhelm. "Implicit Religion and Inter-faith Dialogue: A Philosophical Perspective." *Implicit Religion* 1 (1998) 29–39.

Dupuis, Jacques. *Toward a Christian Theology of Religious Pluralism*. Maryknoll: Orbis, 1997.

Eilers, Franz-Josef, editor. *For All the Peoples of Asia: Federation of Asian Bishops' Conferences*. Vol. 3: *Documents from 1997 to 2001*. Quezon City, Philippines: Claretian, 2002.

Evers, Georg. "Christianity and Harmony: From the Past to the Present." *East Asian Pastoral Review* 29.4 (1992) 348–67.

———. "The Excommunication of Tissa Balasuriya: A Warning to Asian Theologians?" *Jeevadhara* 27 (1997) 212–30.

———. "Recognise the Creativity of the Local Churches." *Jeevadhara* 31.183 (May 2001) 187–92.

Fernandes, Angelo. "Dialogue in the Context of Asian Realities." *Vidyajyoti* 50 (October 1991) 545–60.

Fiorenza, Francis Schüssler. "Systematic Theology: Task and Methods." In *Systematic Theology: Roman Catholic Perspectives*, edited by Francis Schüssler Fiorenza and John P. Galvin, 1:3–87. Minneapolis: Fortress, 1991.

Gadamer, Hans Georg. *Truth and Method*. London: Crossroad, 1975.

Gioia, Francesco, editor. *Interreligious Dialogue: The Official Teaching of the Catholic Church (1963–1995)*. Pontifical Council for Interreligious Dialogue. Boston: Pauline, 1997.

Gispert-Sauch, G. "Reflections around the Case of Fr. Tissa Balasuriya." *Vidyajyoti* 61 (February 1997) 122–25.
Gutierrez, Gustavo. *A Theology of Liberation: History, Politics, and Salvation.* Translated and edited by Sister Caridad Inda and John Eagleson. Maryknoll, NY: Orbis, 1973.
Haight, Roger. "Liberation Theology." In *The New Dictionary of Theology*, edited by Joseph Komonchak, Mary Collins, and Dermot Lane, 570–76. Collegeville, MN: Liturgical, 1987.
Hebblethwaite, Peter. *The New Inquisition?: Schillebeeckx and Kung.* London: Collins, Fount Paperbacks, 1980.
Hefling, Charles. "Method and Meaning in *Dominus Iesus.*" In *Sic et Non: Encountering Dominus Iesus*, edited by Stephen J. Pope and Charles Hefling, 107–23. Maryknoll, NY: Orbis, 2002.
Hill, William. "Human Happiness as God's Honor: Background to a Theology in Transition." In *The Praxis of Christian Experience: An Introduction to the Theology of Edward Schillebeeckx*, edited by Robert Schreiter and Mary Catherine Hilkert, 1–17. San Francisco: Harper & Row, 1989.
"Indians of Various Religions Shocked over 'Unnecessary' Vatican Document." *Union of Catholic Asian News*, 19 September 2000. Online: http://www.ucanews.com/story-archive/?post_name=/2000/09/19/indians-of-various-religions-shocked-over-unnecessary-vatican-document&post_id=16888.
"Japanese Indifferent to '*Dominus Iesus*,' Theologian Regrets Western Approach." *Union of Catholic Asian News*, 5 October 2000. Online: http://www.ucanews.com/story-archive/?post_name=/2000/10/05/japanese-indifferent-to-dominus-iesus-theologian-regrets-western-approach&post_id=16976.
"Justice Denied, Delayed, Truth Exposed: The Inside Story of the Unfair Dealings with J. Dupuis, in a Free-Wheeling Interview Exclusively Given to ICAN." *Indian Currents Associate News*, 15 April 2001, 10–16.
Kennedy, Philip. *Deus Humanissimus: The Knowability of God in the Theology of Edward Schillebeeckx.* Ökumenische Beihefte zur Freiburger Zeitschrift für Philosophie und Theologie 22. Fribourg, Switzerland: University Press, 1993.
———. *Schillebeeckx.* Outstanding Christian Thinkers. London: G. Chapman, 1993.
"Kingdom Value are Core of Church Mission in 21st Century." *Union of Catholic Asian News*, 4 January 2001. Online: http://www.ucanews.com/story-archive/?post_name=/2001/01/04/kingdom-value-are-core-of-church-mission-in-21st-century&post_id=1920.
Komonchak, Joseph. "Vatican Council II." In *The New Dictionary of Theology*, edited by Joseph Komonchak et al., 1072–77. Collegeville, MN: Liturgical, 1987.
Lonergan, Bernard J. F. *Method in Theology.* Toronto: University of Toronto Press, 1971.
McBrien, Richard P. *Catholicism.* Rev. ed. San Francisco: HarperSanFrancisco, 1994.
McCool, Gerald. *Catholic Theology in the Nineteenth Century: The Quest for a Unitary Method.* New York: Seabury, 1977.
———. "Neo-Scholasticism." In *The New Dictionary of Theology*, edited by Joseph Komonchak et al., 713–15. Collegeville, MN: Liturgical, 1987.
McGrath, Alister E. *Christian Theology: An Introduction.* 2nd ed. Oxford: Blackwell, 1997.
"Media Say Vatican Document Threatens Dialogue, Communal Peace." *Union of Catholic Asian News*, 3 October 2000. Online: http://www.ucanews.com/story-archive/?post_name=/2000/10/03/media-say-vatican-document-threatens-dialogue-communal-

peace&post_id=16982.O'Malley, John. *Tradition and Transition: Historical Perspectives on Vatican II*. Delaware: Michael Glazier, 1989.

Menezes, Rui de. "Can Scripture Bail Out *Dominus Jesus*?" *Jeevadhara* 31.183 (May 2001) 209–14.

Mesa, José M. de. "Historical and Cultural Aspects of *Dominus Iesus*." *Jeevadhara* 31.183 (May 2001) 221–23.

Mesa, José M. de, and Lyn L. Wostyn. *Doing Theology: Basic Realities and Processes*. Quezon City, Philippines: Claretian, 1996 [1982].

Painadath, Sebastian. "The Interpersonal and Transpersonal Dimensions of Asian Spirituality." In *FABC Papers No. 83*, 8–16. Hong Kong: FABC, 1997.

Panikkar, Raimon. *The Intrareligious Dialogue*. Rev. ed. New York: Paulist, 1999.

Parappally, Jacob. "Profession and Proclamation of Faith." *Jeevadhara* 31.183 (May 2001) 224–28.

Paul VI, Pope. "*Ecclesiam Suam*: On the Ways in Which the Church Must Carry Out Its Mission in the Contemporary World." August 6, 1964. Online: http://www.vatican.va/holy_father/paul_vi/encyclicals/documents/hf_p-vi_enc_06081964_ecclesiam_en.html.

———. "*Humanae Vitae*: On the Regulation of Birth." July 25, 1968. http://www.vatican.va/holy_father/paul_vi/encyclicals/documents/hf_p-vi_enc_25071968_humanae-vitae_en.html.

Perkins, Pheme. "New Testament Eschatology and *Dominus Iesus*." In *Sic et Non: Encountering Dominus Iesus*, edited by Stephen J. Pope and Charles Hefling, 80–88. Maryknoll, NY: Orbis, 2002.

Pieris, Aloysius. "Asia's Non-Semitic Religions and the Mission of the Local Churches." In *An Asian Theology of Liberation*, 35–50. Quezon City, Philippines: Claretian, 1988.

———. *God's Reign for God's Poor: A Return to the Jesus Formula*. Kelaniya, Sri Lanka: Tulana Research Centre, 1999.

———. "The Roman Catholic Perception of Other Churches and Other Religions after the Vatican's *Dominus Jesus*." *East Asian Pastoral Review* 38.3 (2001) 207–30.

———. "Toward an Asian Theology of Liberation." In *An Asian Theology of Liberation*, 69–86. Faith Meets Faith. Quezon City: Claretians, 1988.

Pontifical Biblical Commission. "The Bible and Christology." In *The Church and the Bible: Official Documents of the Catholic Church*, edited by Dennis J. Murphy, 510–58. Bangalore: Theological Publications in India, 2001.

———. "The Interpretation of the Bible in the Church." In *The Church and the Bible: Official Documents of the Catholic Church*, edited by Dennis J. Murphy, 685–774. Bangalore: Theological Publications in India, 2001.

Pontifical Commission. "Justitia et Pax." *Assise: Journée mondiale de prière pour la paix*, 27 October 1986, 25.

Pope, Stephen J., and Charles Hefling, editors. *Sic et Non: Encountering Dominus Iesus*. Maryknoll, NY: Orbis, 2002.

Portier, William. "Interpretation and Method," In *The Praxis of Christian Experience: An Introduction to the Theology of Edward Schillebeeckx*, edited by Robert J. Schreiter and Mary Catherine Hilkert, 18–34. San Francisco: Harper & Row, 1989.

"Provincials Decry Vatican Suspicion of Asian Theology." *National Catholic Reporter*, 2 April 1999. Online: http://natcath.org/NCR_Online/archives2/1999b/040299/040299i.htm.

Ratzinger, Joseph. "Christ, Faith and the Challenge of Cultures." Given in Hong Kong to the presidents of the Asian Bishops' Conferences and the chairmen of their Doctrinal Commissions, March 2-5, 1993. Online: http://www.ewtn.com/library/curia/ratzhong.htm.

———. "Reasons for the Christian Claim." The remarks made by the Prefect of the Congregation for the Doctrine of the Faith at the presentation of the Church document *Dominus Iesus*, September 5, 2000. Online: http://www.traces-cl.com/archive/2000/ottobre/ratzing.htm.

———. "Relativism: The Central Problem for Faith Today." Address delivered during the meeting of the Congregation for the Doctrine of the Faith with the presidents of the Doctrinal Commissions of the Bishops' Conferences of Latin America. May 1996, Guadalajara, Mexico. Online: http://www.ewtn.com/library/curia/ratzrela.htm.

Robinson, John A. T. *Honest to God*. Philadelphia: Westminster, 1963.

Rosales, Gaudencio B., and Arévalo, C. G., editors. *For All the Peoples of Asia: Federation of Asian Bishops' Conferences*. Vol. 1: *Documents from 1970 to 1991*. Quezon City, Philippines: Claretian, 1992.

Samartha, S. J. *One Christ, Many Religions: Toward a Revised Christology*. Faith Meets Faith. Maryknoll, NY: Orbis, 1991.

Schaeffer, Pamela. "Condemned Priest Is Restored to Church." *National Catholic Reporter*, 30 January 1998. Online: http://natcath.org/NCR_Online/archives2/1998a/013098/bala1.htm.

Schillebeeckx, Edward. *Christ: The Christian Experience in the Modern World*. Translation by John Bowden of *Gerechtigheid en liefde: Genade en bevrijding*. London: SCM, 1980.

———. *Christ the Sacrament of the Encounter with God*. Translation by Paul Barrett of *Christusontmoeting als Sacrament Van de Godsontmoeting*. London: Sheed & Ward, 1963.

———. *Church: The Human Story of God*. Translation by John Bowden of *Mensen als verhaal van God*. New York: Crossroad, 1990.

———. "The Church as the Sacrament of Dialogue." In *God the Future of Man*, translation by N. D. Smith of *Gott die Zukunft des Menschen*, 117–40. New York: Sheed & Ward, 1968.

———. "Epilogue: The New Image of God, Secularization and Man's Future on Earth." In *God the Future of Man*, translation by N. D. Smith of *Gott die Zukunft des Menschen*, 167–203. New York: Sheed & Ward, 1968.

———. *God Is New Each Moment: Edward Schillebeeckx in Conversation with Huub Oosterhuis and Piet Hoogeveen*. Translation by David Smith of *God is ieder ogenblik nieuw*. New York: Seabury, 1983.

———. *I Am a Happy Theologian: Conversations with Francesco Strazzari*. Translation of *Sono un teologo felice*. New York: Crossroad, 1994.

———. *Interim Report on the Books "Jesus" & "Christ."* Translation by John Bowden of *Tussentijds verhaal over twee Jezus boeken*. London: SCM, 1980.

———. *Jesus: An Experiment in Christology*. Translation by Hubert Hoskins of *Jezus het verhaal van een levende*. New York: Collins and Crossroad, 1979.

———. "The Religious and the Human Ecumene." In *The Language of Faith: Essays on Jesus, Theology, and the Church*, 256–57. Maryknoll, NY: Orbis, 1995.

———. "Secularization and Christian Belief in God." In *God the Future of Man*, translation by N. D. Smith of *Gott die Zukunft des Menschen*, 51–90. New York: Sheed & Ward, 1968.

———. "Towards a Catholic Use of Hermeneutics." In *God the Future of Man*, translation by N. D. Smith of *Gott die Zukunft des Menschen*, 1–50. New York: Sheed & Ward, 1968.

———. *The Understanding of Faith: Interpretation and Criticism*. Translation by N. D. Smith of *Geloofsverstaan*. London: Sheed & Ward, 1974.

Schoof, T. M. *Breakthrough: Beginnings of the New Catholic Theology*. Translation by N. D. Smith of *Aggiornamento*. Dublin: Gilland Macmillan, 1970.

———. "E. Schillebeeckx: 25 years in Nijmegen." *Theology Digest* 37.4 (Winter 1990) 313–32.

———. "Masters in Israel: VII. The Later Theology of Edward Schillebeeckx. The New Position of Theology After Vatican II." *The Clergy Review* 55.12 (December 1970) 943–60.

———, editor. *The Schillebeeckx Case: Official Exchange of Letters and Documents in the Investigation of Fr. Edward Schillebeeckx by the Sacred Congregation for the Doctrine of the Faith, 1976–1980*. Translation by Matthew J. O'Connell of *De Zaak Schillebeeckx*. New York: Paulist, 1984.

Schreiter, Robert J. "In Memoriam Edward Schillebeeckx (1914–2009)." No pages. Online: http://schillebeeckx.nl/overlijden-edward-schillebeeckx/in-memoriam.

———, editor. *The Schillebeeckx Reader*. New York: Crossroad, 1984.

Schweitzer, Albert. *The Quest for the Historical Jesus: A Critical Study of Its Progress from Reimarus to Wrede*. London: A. & C. Black, 1954.

"Some Church People Regret Vatican Language, Others Justify Recent *Declaration*." *Union of Catholic Asian News*, 14 September 2000. Online: http://www.ucanews.com/story-archive/?post_name=/2000/09/14/some-church-people-regret-vatican-language-others-justify-recent-declaration&post_id=16834.

Standing Committee of the Catholic Bishops' Conference of India. "Pastoral Guidelines on the Writings of Late Fr. Tony de Mello." *Vidyajyoti* 63 (August 1999) 605–11.

"Statement by the Institute of Missiology Missio, Aachen regarding the Excommunication of Fr. Tissa Balasuriya OMI." *Vidyajyoti* 61 (February 1997) 120–22.

"Theology Institute Initiates Public Discussion on '*Dominus Iesus*.'" *Union of Catholic Asian News*, 29 December 2000. Online: http://www.ucanews.com/story-archive/?post_name=/2000/12/29/theology-institute-initiates-public-discussion-on-dominus-iesus&post_id=17488.

Thurlings, J. M. G. "Pluralism and Assimilation in the Netherlands, with Special Reference to Dutch Catholicism." *International Journal of Comparative Sociology* 20.1–2 (1979) 82–100.

Tomko, Josef. "Proclaiming Christ the World's Only Savior." *L'Osservatore Romano*, 5 April 1991, 4.

Wilfred, Felix. "Towards a Better Understanding of Asian Theology." *Vidyajyoti* 62 (December 1998) 890–915.

———. "The Federation of Asian Bishops' Conferences (FABC): Orientations, Challenges and Impact." In *For All the People of Asia: Federation of Asian Bishops' Conferences*, vol. 1: *Documents from 1970 to 1991*, edited by Gaudencio Rosales and C. G. Arevalo, xxiii–xxx. Quezon City, Philippines: Claretian, 1992.

———. "Liberating Dialogue." In *From the Dusty Soil: Contextual Reinterpretation of Christianity*, 261–74. Asian Theological Search 4. Madras: University of Madras, 1995.

———. "Towards a Theology of Harmony." *Jarbuch für kontextuelle Theologien* (*Yearbook of Contextual Theologies*), 1993, 146–58.

Zaner, Richard M., and Don Ihde. *Phenomenology and Existentialism*. New York: Putnam, 1973.

www.ingramcontent.com/pod-product-compliance
Lightning Source LLC
Chambersburg PA
CBHW050815160426
43192CB00010B/1769